Maintaining Function in Older Adults

Linda A. Newman, P.T.

.

Butterworth-Heinemann

Boston   Oxford   Melbourne   Singapore   Toronto   Munich
New Delhi   Tokyo

Every effort has been made to ensure that the drug dosage schedules within this text are accurate and conform to standards accepted at time of publi-cation. However, as treatment recommendations vary in the light of con-tinuing research and clinical experience, the reader is advised to verify drug dosage schedules herein with information found on product information sheets. This is especially true in cases of new or infrequently used drugs.

 Recognizing the importance of preserving what has been written, Butter-worth- Heinemann prints its books on acid-free paper whenever possible.

Library of Congress Cataloging-in-Publication Data
Newman, Linda A., 1943–
   Maintaining function in older adults / Linda A. Newman.
     p. cm.
   ISBN 0-7506-9568-4 (alk. paper)
   1. Physical therapy for the aged. 2. Aged, Physically
handicapped—Rehabilitation. I. Title
   [DNLM: 1. Physical Therapy—in old age. 2. Exercise Therapy—in
old age. 3. Aging—physiology. 4. Activities of Daily Living.
   5. Aged—psychology. WB 460 N553m 1995]
RC953.8.P58N48 1995
615.8'2'0846—dc20
DNLM/DLC
for Library of Congress   95-13936
                                              CIP

British Library Cataloguing-in-Publication Data
A catalogue record for this book is available from the British Library.

The publisher offers discounts on bulk orders of this book.
For information, please write:
Manager of Special Sales
Butterworth-Heinemann
313 Washington Street
Newton, MA 02158-1626

10 9 8 7 6 5 4 3 2 1

Printed in the United States of America

Contents

Maintaining Function
in Older Adults

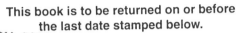

Dedicated to the memory of my father, Henry Smets

Acknowledgments

I appreciate the help of Michael Moran, Sc.D., P.T., and John M. Barbis, M.A., P.T., O.C.S., who reviewed the manuscript and offered many very valuable suggestions, and Kevin B. Newman and Margaret Hughes, who assisted with the photographs. Most of all, I am grateful for the help of my husband, Boyd E. Newman. Boyd did all the work of compiling the photographs and was a constant source of encouragement and advice.

Key Words

Exercise prescription, fall prevention, functional outcome, managed care, mobility, prevention, quality assurance, total quality management

1

Introduction

This handbook is for physical therapists who provide services to older people in nursing homes, adult day care centers, personal care homes, and long-term care rehabilitation units. It describes an approach to maintaining a patient's functional status and preventing further disability. The therapist organizes and constructs the program, evaluates patients for inclusion, and prescribes exercises based on the evaluation. The therapist instructs group leaders in the exercise procedures described, supervises the overall program, and periodically reevaluates the goals and progress of participants.

PREVENTION AND MAINTENANCE

Prevention of disability has always been important to physical therapy practice. A mother of a child with cerebral palsy is taught handling techniques to facilitate normal muscle tone and prevent contractures. An athlete recovering from an anterior cruciate ligament reconstruction is taught strengthening exercises for the quadriceps and hamstring muscles. A visiting therapist instructs family members in an exercise program in the home for a person who has experienced a stroke.

An older person with a disability may benefit from a continuing program of exercise and mobility to maintain function and prevent additional loss of independence.

MUSCULOSKELETAL, SENSORIMOTOR, AND CARDIOPULMONARY CHANGES WITH AGING

Some changes in the musculoskeletal system are a normal part of aging, but they may result in disability in an older person. A gradual loss of strength occurs. This decrease is greater in the back and proximal muscles of the lower extremities and less in the upper extremities.[1] A decrease in flexibility may lead to contractures of the hip flexor muscles and dorsal kyphosis. Rigidity of the proximal muscles of the back and hips leads to back pain and results in postural changes and a decline in the ability to respond rapidly to the forces of gravity. Thinning of the intervertebral disks with formation of osteophytes and other arthritic changes contribute to back pain and loss of mobility. With age, there is also gradual bone loss, which accelerates after the age of 50 years, and a greater risk of fractures.[1-3]

Age-related sensorimotor changes can contribute to disability. Vision and hearing decline with age.[1,2,4] Meniere's disease can affect the vestibular system and cause balance and hearing loss. Osteoarthritis of the feet, ankles, or knees not only causes pain during ambulation but also interferes with proprioceptive signals, affecting the normal biomechanics of the joints.[5] Proprioceptive input also may be altered by edema of the ankles or knees. Edema may be caused by impaired circulatory function, by a decrease in kidney function, or by inflammation secondary to arthritic changes.

A decrease in proprioception impedes the postural alignments necessary to maintain balance. The feedback mechanism between the visual, vestibular, and proprioceptive systems is critical for balance. There is evidence that reduced proprioception and vestibular and somatosensory function occur with increased age and may contribute to falls.[6-8]

These musculoskeletal and sensorimotor changes affect both static and dynamic balance. Gait alterations include a lower amplitude and speed of movement, shorter steps, wider base of support, and increased double support time. Postural sway also tends to increase with age.[2,4]

The cardiovascular and pulmonary systems also undergo changes with age.[1,2] Atherosclerotic changes in the cerebral arteries can cause hypotension with position changes. Atherosclerosis may affect the vestibular system. This is especially important during transfers from supine to sitting and sitting to standing. Degenerative changes in the cervical vertebrae among the elderly may cause disruption of the blood flow of the vertebral artery. Symptoms include vertigo and blurred vision, especially when extending, rotating, or laterally flexing the neck. These movements typically occur during transfers, such as rising to stand or turning the head to locate a chair to prepare to sit.

Cardiac changes include myocardial stiffness, irregular cardiac rhythm, and alterations in blood pressure and heart rate response. Pulmonary changes make it more difficult for the lungs to supply oxygen to exercising muscles.[3] A decrease in endurance results from a decline in muscle endurance and aerobic capacity. These are normal changes in aging, but they are likely to affect the ability to make rapid adjustments in cardiac output during exercise and activities of daily living (ADL).

All these factors place older people, especially if they already have a disability, at risk for additional decline in function or for falls.

RESEARCH SUPPORT FOR INTERVENTION TO IMPROVE FUNCTIONAL OUTCOMES IN OLDER ADULTS

Recent research demonstrates the effectiveness of exercise for the elderly (including those in assisted living settings) in strength,[9-12] gait, and balance,[13-17] ADL,[1,18,19] memory,[20] neuropsychologic functioning,[21] and even life satisfaction.[22] Regular exercise has been shown to reduce cardiovascular risk[23] and result in improved functional performance, even in patients with cardiac disease.[24] Weight-bearing exercise has the additional benefit of preventing osteoporosis.[25,26] A recent study confirmed that a regular group exercise program, planned and supervised by a physical therapist, is safe and improves physical functioning in frail, elderly people who live in institutions.[27] In addition, such a program is a cost-effective use of a therapist's time.[28,29]

INDICATIONS FOR A PREVENTION PROGRAM FOR OLDER ADULTS

Older people receiving long-term care, assisted living, or adult day care may need a maintenance or prevention program, especially those who

1. Without intervention are at risk for further disability, or injury, such as falls
2. Have a cognitive or psychiatric disability concurrent with a physical disability, which results in an inability to carry through with an independent program

CHAPTER SUMMARIES

Working in groups is a cost-effective way to provide services. It stimulates social interaction and provides enjoyment to patients. In the case reports that appear throughout this book, patients described as participating in group exercises were able to do all of the suggested activities, although sometimes with cues and assistance. When a patient was unable to perform some exercises, or when some were especially effective, the circumstances are described. These case reports serve to illustrate how a patient may require skilled physical therapy services only intermittently, yet may benefit from an ongoing program to maintain his or her level of functional independence.

Chapters 2 and 3 describe a variety of therapeutic exercises and their rationale for use. These activities can be used in working with patients in small groups (Figure 1–1). It is helpful to divide the patients into groups according to their ability to walk. Maintaining ambulatory and transfer skills is em-

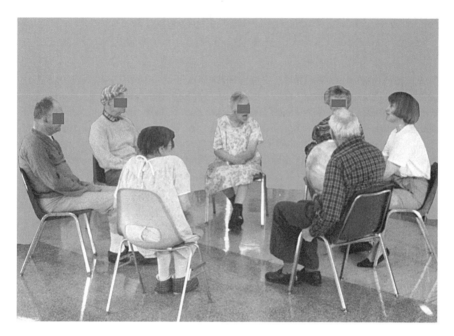

Figure 1-1 An exercise group.

phasized in an ambulatory group; wheelchair skills, upper extremity range of motion, and strengthening are the focus for a nonambulatory group.

Chapters 4 through 6 discuss cardiovascular and pulmonary conditioning, exercises for a patient with a shoulder disability, and activities for a person with a severe cognitive impairment or positioning needs.

Chapter 7, on communication and motivation, contains suggestions for working with patients in groups. It also discusses problems of patient cooperation, working with a disruptive patient, and an effective approach to a confused person.

Chapter 8 discusses falls and their prevention. Falls often result in fractures of the hip, skull, distal radius, and proximal humerus and are a leading cause of disability and death among the elderly. Physical therapists are in a unique position to address this problem. We consider various interventions, including mobility and balance testing, environmental assessment, and evaluation of fall risk. A case report illustrates how therapists can evaluate for the risk of falls and recommend useful interventions to caregivers, even when the patient is unable to benefit directly from an exercise program. The chapter also discusses how restraints are often used in an effort to prevent falls and provides some practical, safe alternatives to the use of restraints.

Chapter 9 considers administration of a prevention program in terms of meeting patient and facility goals. It reviews the important effects of medications on patient treatment. The chapter also discusses quality assurance from a customer-oriented viewpoint and offers quality assessment indicators, including some that specifically apply to maintaining function in group programs.

Therapists often define levels of guarding and assistance and cues differently. The system used in this book is described in Appendix A. Conventions describing disablement, joint motion, and muscle strength are included in Appendices B through D. Concerning gender, for convenience the patient is sometimes referred to as male and the therapist as female. The information applies equally to the female patient and male therapist.

REFERENCES

1. Mount J. Designing exercise programs for the elderly. In: Rothman J, Levine R, eds. *Prevention practice: Strategies in physical therapy and occupational therapy.* Philadelphia: Saunders, 1992, pp.218–233.
2. Lewis CB, Bottomley JM. *Geriatric physical therapy: A clinical approach.* Norwalk: Appleton & Lange, 1994.
3. Skinner JS. Importance of aging for exercise testing and exercise prescription. In Skinner JS. *Exercise testing and exercise prescription for special cases: Theoretical basis and clinical application,* 2d ed. Philadelphia: Lea & Febiger, 1993, pp. 75–86.
4. May BJ. Principles of exercise for the elderly. In: Basmajian JV, Wolf SL, eds. *Therapeutic exercise,* 5th ed. Baltimore: Williams & Wilkins, 1990, pp. 279–298.
5. Marks R, Quinney HA, Wessel J. Proprioceptive sensibility in women with normal and osteoarthritic knee joints. *Clin Rheumatol* 1993;12:170–175.
6. Lord SR, Webster IW. Visual field dependence in elderly fallers and non fallers. *Int J Aging Hum Dev* 1990;31:267–277.
7. Teasdale N, Stelmach GE, Breunig A. Postural sway characteristics of the elderly under normal and altered visual and support surface conditions. *J Gerontol* 1991;46:B238–B244.
8. Yamaguchi S, Knight RT. Age effects on the P300 to novel somatosensory stimuli. *Electroencephalogr Clin Neurophysiol* 1991;78:297–301.
9. Fiatarone MA, Marks EC, Ryan ND, Meredith CN, Lipsitz LA, Evans WJ. High intensity strength training in nonagenarians: Effects on skeletal muscle. *JAMA* 1990;263:3029–3034.
10. Pyka G, Lindenberger E, Charette S, Marcus R. Muscle strength and fiber adaptations to a year-long resistance training program in elderly men and women. *J Gerontol* 1994;49:M22–M27.
11. Dupler TL, Cortes C. Effects of a whole body resistive training regimen in the elderly. *Gerontology* 1993;39:314–319.
12. Fitarone MA, O'Neill EF, Ryan ND, et al. Exercise training and nutritional supplementation for physical frailty in very elderly people. *N Engl J Med* 1994;330:1769–1775.
13. Judge JO, Lindsey C, Underwood M, Winsemius D. Balance improvements in older women: Effects of exercise training. *Phys Ther* 1993;73:254–265.

14. Sauvage LR Jr, Myklebust BM, Criw-Pan J, et al. A clinical trial of strengthening and aerobic exercise to improve gait and balance in elderly male nursing home residents. *Am J Phys Med Rehabil* 1992;71:333–342.
15. Conright KC, Evans JP, Nassralla SM, Tran MV, Silver AJ, Morley JE. A walking program improves gait and balance in nursing home patients (letter). *J Am Geriatr Soc* 1990;38:1267.
16. Hu M, Woollacott MH. Multisensory training of standing balance in older adults. I. Postural stability and one leg stance balance. *J Gerontol* 1994;49:M52–M61.
17. Hu M, Woollacott MH. Multisensory training of standing balance in older adults. II. Kinematic and electromyographic postural responses. *J Gerontol* 1994;49:M62–M71.
18. Mulrow CD, Gerety MB, Kanten D, et al. A randomized trial of physical rehabilitation for very frail nursing home residents. *JAMA* 1994;271:519–524.
19. Wolfson L, Whipple R, Judge J, Amerman P, Derby C, King M. Training balance and strength in the elderly to improve function. *J Am Geriatr Soc* 1993;11:341–343.
20. Stones MJ, Dawe D. Acute exercise facilitates semantically cued memory in nursing home residents. *J Am Geriatr Soc* 1993;41:531–534.
21. Molloy DW, Beerschoten DA, Borrie MJ, Crilly RG, Cape RD. Acute effects of exercise on neuropsychological function in elderly subjects. *J Am Geriatr Soc* 1988;36:29–33.
22. Topp R, Stevenson JS. The effects of attendance and effort on outcomes among older adults in a long term exercise program. *Res Nurs Health* 1994;17:15–24.
23. Shepard RJ. The scientific basis of exercise prescribing for the very old. *J Am Geriatr Soc* 1990;38:62–70.
24. Anderson JM. Rehabilitating elderly cardiac patients. *West J Med* 1991;154:573–578.
25. Hatori M, Hasegawa A, Adachi H, Shinozaki A. The effects of walking at the anaerobic threshold level on vertebral bone loss in postmenopausal women. *Calcif Tissue Int* 1993;52:411–414.
26. Aisenbrey JA. Exercise in the prevention and management of osteoporosis. *Phys Ther* 1987;67:1100–1104.
27. Chiodo LK, Gerety MB, Mulrow CD, Rhodes MC, Tuley MR. The impact of physical therapy on nursing home patient outcomes. *Phys Ther* 1992;72:168–175.
28. O'Hagan CM, Smith DM, Pileggi KL. Exercises classes in rest homes: Effect on physical function. *N Z Med J* 1994;107:39–40.
29. Bider J. Group exercise for frail elderly. *J Aging Phys Act* 1994;2:25–37.

2

Exercises for a Group of Ambulatory Patients: With or Without Assistive Devices

Patients may walk with supervision as needed from their rooms or units or the lobby. Patients who typically use a wheelchair should transfer to a regular chair for the session. Chairs should be firm with a straight back (not lounge or easy chairs). Patients who can come to standing with supervision only do not need armrests on the chairs. Patients who need assistance to stand should use chairs with armrests. Teach the patients to come to standing by pushing on the armrests. Patients should wear well fitting, supportive shoes (not slippers). They should be dressed. Patients should wear a gait belt for safety or a waistband or belt on their clothing. Patients should wear glasses and hearing aids, if needed.

The environment is important for comfort, communication, and safety. Lighting should be bright, but there should be no glare. Eliminate background noise as much as possible. Closing windows and doors may decrease noise. The floor may be carpeted (flat carpeting, not shag or deep pile) or tiled; wax should be nonskid and nonglare. Patients sit in a circle approximately 20 feet in diameter.

TRANSFER TRAINING

Teach the patients correct and safe transfer techniques. From sitting to standing, direct the participants to move their buttocks forward in the chair, allowing their knees to flex 90 to 110 degrees. Participants should place one or both hands on the edge of the chair or armrest; one hand may be placed on the walker or cane, if the patient uses one (Figure 2–1). Patients should not place both hands on the walker or cane. If they do, you need to stabilize the device to prevent it from tipping and will not have both hands free to guard the patients. Instruct the patients to lean forward from the hips to

Figure 2–1 The patient flexes the stronger (left) knee, leans forward slightly, and prepares to push to a standing position with her right hand on the chair.

bring their center of gravity over the feet, keeping the head forward (Figures 2–2 and 2–3). No one should extend his or her head, or the center of gravity will not move forward enough. Instruct participants to push up from the chair, extending their knees and hips.

People guarding patients ideally should not touch them at all. Many patients have come to expect a boost up and do not exert full effort if they are touched. If a patient needs physical cues or assistance, analyze which component of the transfer is deficient. The person can then practice the component and integrate it into the goal of rising from the chair.[1] Perhaps he only needs assistance to move the buttocks forward or a verbal or physical cue to keep the head forward. If a patient lacks sufficient strength in the quadriceps, gluteals, or upper extremity muscles, strengthening exercises should be emphasized in the program. In the meantime, you may have to assist the patient, either by grasping her belt or holding her under the arm. Provide only the amount of assistance the patient actually needs; patients usually need assistance only in the first half of the transfer.

One would think transfers from standing to sitting would be easier, but they are often more difficult because of the motor planning involved. The person must approach the chair, turn around completely and then back up, bringing the cane or walker with him. Many elderly people lack sufficient

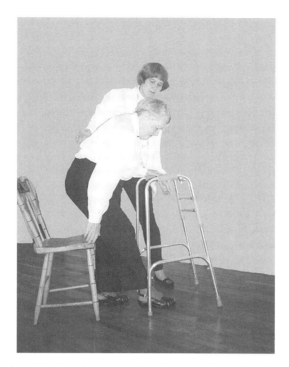

Figure 2–2   As the patient rises, her center of gravity moves forward over her feet.

Figure 2–3   Standing erect with both hands on the walker, the patient holds her head erect and shoulders back.

9

trunk and cervical rotation, or they have visual deficits that prevent them from seeing the position of the chair before sitting. Instruct the patient to back up completely, until his thighs contact the edge of the chair (Figures 2–4 and 2–5). He then removes his hand from the walker and reaches backward for the chair. The procedure is reversed from sitting to standing; the patient bends forward at the hips, keeping the head forward, and lowers himself slowly into the chair by bending the knees. Discourage the person from flopping.

Many patients may have forgotten how to safely transfer from standing to sitting. Staff members sometimes contribute to the problem by using a wheelchair to scoop up a patient who is standing. Many patients thus learn to just sit and depend on someone else to have a chair ready to receive them. Demonstration and example can be used to informally educate caregivers in how to cue patients in safe technique.

GAIT TRAINING

For a person walking across a room or in the hall, provide only the amount of assistance, contact guarding, or supervision that she actually needs. Do not hold the person's hand because your hands will not be free to

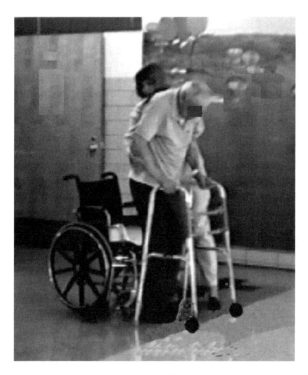

Figure 2–4   The patient backs up until the back of his knees contact the edge of the wheelchair seat.

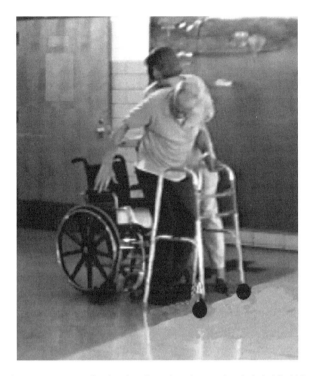

Figure 2–5   The patient rotates his head and trunk to locate the chair behind him and reaches back for the armrest of the wheelchair to prepare to sit.

control her trunk and help her maintain balance, if needed. If necessary, touch the patient lightly at the waist or hips and stay very close, beside and slightly behind the person. Do not allow the person to lean on you. If she is unable to stand without support, the patient may need a walker or other assistive device to walk.

In the descriptions that follow, *pushing a wheelchair* means the patient is sitting in the wheelchair, propelling it. Sometimes a patient is encouraged to walk with the wheelchair, pushing it in front. However, a wheelchair pushed in this way cannot be safely maneuvered around obstacles and is too large to take into a bathroom. A wheeled walker is preferable.

Sometimes a patient is not a functional ambulator, although he can transfer and walk safely, because his pace is too slow. Either it takes him too long to come to standing, or he walks too slowly to, for example, get to the bathroom in time. The person should walk at a pace that feels comfortable to him, which is consistent with his strength, balance, and coordination. It does not help to ask the person to "hurry up." Asking a person to exceed his limits by walking faster is dangerous and can lead to falls. Exercises directed at correcting deficiencies in technique or improving strength, range of motion, and endurance should allow the patient's pace to increase to a functional level. A patient who walks too fast, sometimes carrying the walker or cane, is often using an assistive device that is inappropriate for him. Reevaluate for the appropriate assistive device. When the device is fitted properly, the patient walks with greater safety and uses the assistive device correctly.

Following are some suggested exercises and activities that address various components of transfers, gait, balance, coordination, muscle strength, and range of motion. They also reinforce cognitive skills.

TRANSFER AND GAIT ACTIVITIES

Trading Chairs

The group forms a circle 15 to 20 feet in diameter. Add two additional chairs. Ask each person in turn to stand, walk across the circle, turn, and sit down while you provide the appropriate level of assistance, guarding, or supervision. Emphasize safe technique and correct use of assistive devices, while providing only the level of assistance needed, to encourage independence. Add instructions to stop suddenly—"Freeze!"—to promote increased speed of reaction and postural control.

Carrying Objects

Hand a cap, scarf, necklace, or bracelet to a patient, who may be standing or seated. Ask her to put it on, then walk across the circle, take it off, hand it to another person, then turn and return to his seat. This activity involves using the upper extremities while maintaining standing balance and turning 180 degrees in place. The person learns to follow three- and four-step commands and develop motor planning skills.

Uneven Surfaces

The foregoing activities are made more challenging by varying the surface, using a foam pad or mat on the floor, or walking outside, on the sidewalk, grass, or gravel. Uneven surfaces facilitate the postural adjustments and motor control necessary for balance.[1]

Obstacle Course

Ask each person to stand, walk across the circle and around another chair or obstacle, then walk back to his seat. This will be a challenging activity for people with cognitive deficits because it involves multistep commands. To make it more difficult, ask the participant to retrieve an object, give it to another person, and then return to his seat. You can also construct a slalom or obstacle course with strategically placed bleach bottles, quad canes, or chairs to maneuver around.

Races

Ask two patients with similar ability to race each other across the room or around an obstacle, such as a chair. It helps to turn the chair over, otherwise a patient may sit down on it! Guard both contestants. Use runoff heats as needed. Be sure to congratulate both winners and losers for a good effort.

Chair-to-Floor Transfers

Place a mat at least 4 x 6 feet in area on the floor with patients seated around it. Begin by showing the participants how to get down on the floor, lie down on the back, and then get up again. Show several different methods. Help the most able of the group down to the mat, and ask her to get up (Figures 2–6 and 2–7). This is a difficult and advanced motor challenge, and you need to allow enough time for the person to devise his own strategy. One person may roll from supine to prone, then to quadruped to crawl to a chair, then to kneeling and half kneeling, and turn to sit (Figures 2–8 and 2–9). Another may push up to sitting position, back up to a chair, place his hands on the seat of the chair behind him, and use shoulder depression and elbow extension to lift his buttocks to the seat.

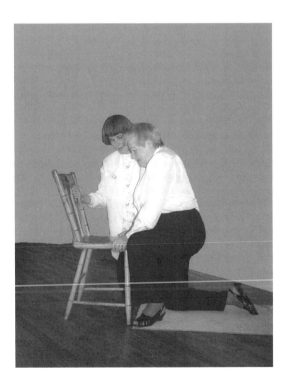

Figure 2–6 The patient moves from kneeling to half-kneeling, using a chair for support.

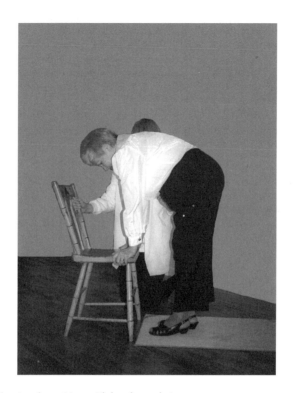

Figure 2–7 Plantigrade position with hands on chair seat.

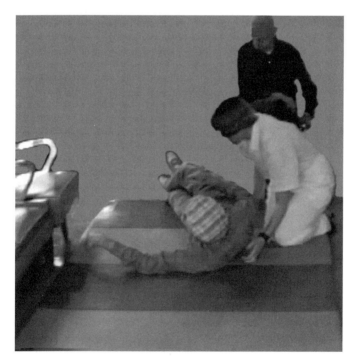

Figure 2–8 The patient is cued to roll from supine.

14

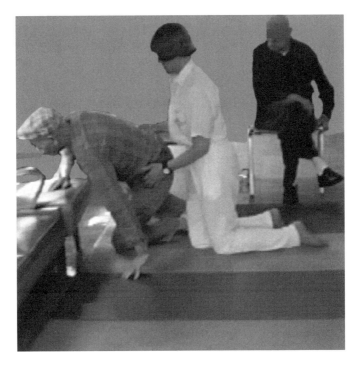

Figure 2–9 The patient moves to kneeling, using a chair for support.

Guard the person closely throughout this maneuver, especially the head, and do not try to rush the patient or provide assistance until it is very clear he needs it (Figures 2–10 through 2–14). It is usually more difficult to help a person to the floor than to guard or assist him getting up. Assist each participant to perform the maneuver and discuss how the person is performing the activity as he or she does it; this teaches the others in the group. Some people in the group may be physically or cognitively unable to perform this activity.

Car Transfers

Instruct members of the group, one at a time, to get in and out of a car. Each person learns technique by observing the others. In cool weather, include donning and doffing hats and coats and encourage independence in that activity.

Elevations

It may be argued that in protected environments, people do not need to learn to use curbs, steps, or ramps. These activities can be valuable, however, for the development of strength, range of motion, and motor planning. De-

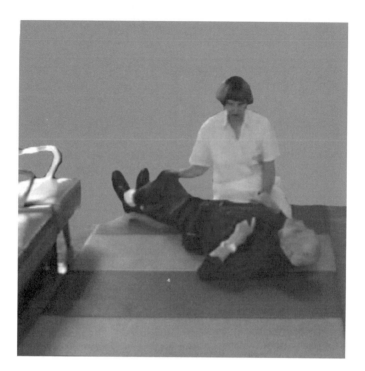

Figure 2–10 Patient supine.

Figure 2–11 Patient rolls to side-lying with weight on forearm through shoulder.

16

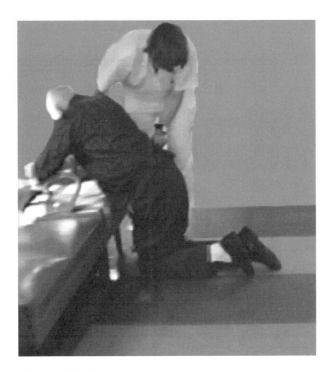

Figure 2–12   High kneeling with contact guard.

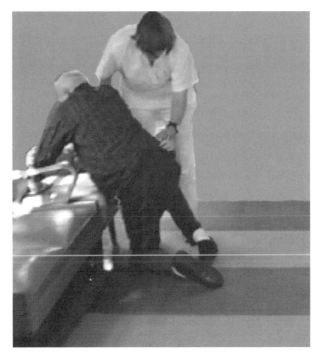

Figure 2–13   With verbal and physical cues, patient moves to half-kneeling position.

Figure 2–14 Patient requires moderate assistance to turn to sitting in chair.

veloping improved mobility in all situations leads to increased feelings of competence. In addition, there may be a need to evacuate the building in an emergency, and elevators may not be operating.

Curbs and Steps

Use one or two railings initially; then, if possible, progress to no railings. A walker can substitute for a railing at a curb. For correct sequencing, determine which lower extremity is weaker. Lead with the stronger leg ascending and the weaker descending. Later, progress to foot-over-foot sequencing.

If your facility does not have a curb, use a low, wide stool, or a wooden or heavy plastic soft-drink box, approximately 18 inches long by 13 wide by 5 inches high. These are usually available for the price of a deposit. Height-adjustable steps, used for step aerobics classes, also can be used.

Ramps

Ramps should not have more than 5 degrees of incline, or 1 inch of rise for every foot of length. People with limitations in ankle range of motion (ROM) or balance deficits may have difficulty with ramps. If possible, use a railing on one or both sides initially. Activities with ramps may include side-stepping with both hands on the railing and walking backward, which facilitates ankle control and flexibility. Descending an incline also requires eccentric control of the quadriceps and tibialis anterior muscles.

STANDING BALANCE AND POSTURE CONTROL

Throwing and Catching a Ball

A Koosh (ODDzOn Products, Campbell, Calif 95009 (408) 379-3906; available in toy stores) or other ball that does not roll or bounce is easiest to handle. This activity requires two group leaders, one to guard the patient and one to throw the ball. If the participant uses a walker or cane, move it off to the side if possible while the facilitator provides contact guarding. Instruct the patient to stand with feet apart, one foot slightly ahead of the other. Vary the difficulty of this exercise by moving to various positions to throw the ball, encouraging the participants to use trunk rotation. Moving closer or farther away allows the participant to judge distances. Throwing overhand or sidearm and throwing and catching with the nonpreferred hand also increase the difficulty.

Encourage the patient to pick up the ball from the floor, if possible, although this may provoke vertigo for people with vestibular disturbances. If a participant is prone to vertigo, ask him to pick up the ball from a chair or table surface. Participants may also throw the ball to each other, while the facilitators provide the necessary guarding to them both. Some participants may be able to stand and dribble a ball (Figure 2–15).

Throwing Bean Bags

Throw bean bags to a target, such as into a chair, onto a table, or into a wastebasket (Figure 2–16). Vary the difficulty by altering the distance, position, or size of the target. Placing the target to the side facilitates trunk rotation. It may be fun to keep score; however, everyone should have a feeling of success, so try to ensure a score of at least 75 percent.

One Foot (Static) Standing Balance

Ask the participant to lift one foot off the floor and hold it up, using her usual assistive device. Note the number of seconds she maintains standing balance to record progress.

Dynamic Balance

Have the participant stand 6 to 12 inches from a wall, facing it. He holds his hands at chest level and leans into the wall, then pushes away, regaining upright stance. This may also be done sideways with right or left shoulder

Figure 2–15 A patient dribbling a ball. Therapist provides close supervision.

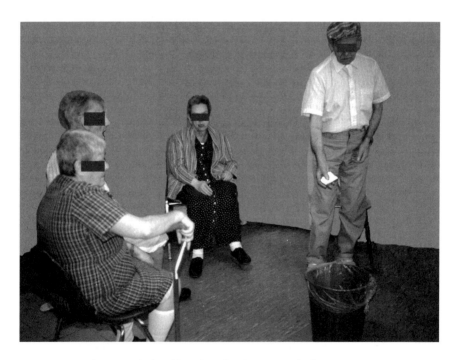

Figure 2–16 The patient is throwing a bean bag into a wastebasket.

leaning into the wall, and the patient uses his hand to push away. A more advanced exercise is to face away from the wall, lean backward against it, and use trunk and head flexion to lean forward and regain upright standing.

This activity facilitates protective extension reflexes,[1] which prevent head injury in a fall. Many older people have a fear of falling, which makes this exercise particularly challenging. However, when mastered, and with repetition, the patient's confidence improves.

Forward-backward Stepping

Have the person stand facing a wall or chair and place his hands on the wall or chair. The participant steps forward, backward, to the right, and to the left. This activity reinforces motor planning and concepts of directionality. It is especially useful for people who have difficulty backing up to a chair.

Rope Activities

Jump Rope

Two participants sit in chairs and hold a 6-foot rope between them, laying it on the floor. Direct the other patients to lift their assistive devices and step over it (Figures 2–17 and 2–18). As each patient is able, raise the rope

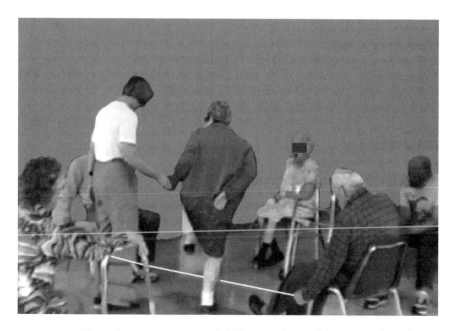

Figure 2–17 The patient steps over a rope held by two other participants. The therapist provides contact guarding.

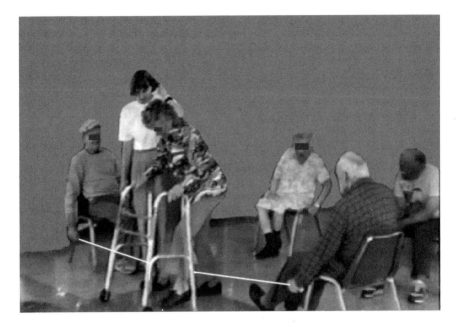

Figure 2–18   The patient lifts her walker and steps over the rope.

in 1- to 2-inch increments. This activity challenges the visual motor system, balance, and coordination.

Limbo Stick or Rope

Two participants sitting on chairs hold an 8- to 10-foot dowel rod or a rope as high as possible. Other participants do the limbo under the stick or rope, using cervical ROM to duck their heads (Figure 2–19). Leaning backward is not necessary! The rope or stick holders must exercise co-contraction of the shoulder girdle muscles, and the limbo dancers use visual perceptual skills.

POSTURAL EXERCISES

1. Chin tucks. Keeping the eyes level, bring the head straight back. Sometimes it helps to place a finger gently on the chin and press back. This can be a difficult exercise to learn; avoid overextension of the cervical spine.

2. Cervical exercises. Look to the right, left, up, and down slowly, while keeping the eyes open. Repeat with eyes closed while being guarded. Patients with cervical degenerative disease or Ménière's disease are at risk for vertigo during this exercise.

3. Scapular retraction. Pinch your shoulder blades together or clasp your hands together behind the back at the buttocks, and with elbows straight, reach backward.

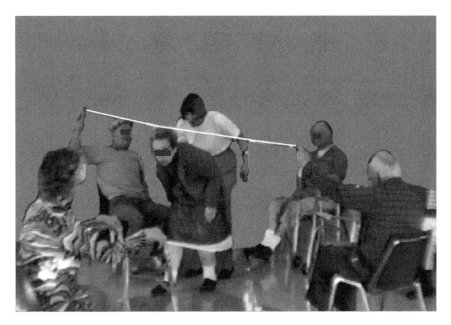

Figure 2–19 A patient ducks under a rope held high by two other participants.

4. Scapular exercises. Lift the shoulders, then pull shoulders backward, down, and forward. The verbal cue, "Pretend there's a pencil at the end of your shoulder, now draw a circle with it," simplifies the instruction.

5. Shoulder horizontal abduction. Lace the fingers together behind the neck, and push the elbows back.

6. Lumbar range of motion. Alternately flatten the lower back, then (gently) arch the back. The movement should be slow, smooth, and controlled. Practice simple cervical and trunk movements first in a sitting position, then standing, if possible. Hold each position for 5 seconds before releasing. Breathe during the exercise.

7. Balance. Walk with a small, floppy 14-inch square pillow balanced on your head. To balance the pillow, you automatically keep your head up, hold abdomen in, and keep shoulders back (Figures 2–20 and 2–21).

GROSS MOTOR COORDINATION, STRENGTHENING, RANGE OF MOTION

Kicking a Ball

Suspend a tetherball by a cord from the ceiling at ankle height, and ask the participants to kick it. Walkers are put to one side. The participant places one hand on the walker, and the facilitator provides contact guarding on the other side. Make the activity more difficult by asking the participants

Figure 2–20   The patient concentrates on keeping his head erect and shoulders back.

Figure 2–21   The patient balances the pillow on his head while standing with the walker. The therapist provides contact guarding.

to kick with the nonpreferred foot. Still more difficult is to have two participants kick a ball to each other.

Standing Exercises

Other exercises in a standing position include marching in place, half knee bends, swinging a leg forward with heel strike in front and toe off behind, and knee flexion in standing. These are effective exercises for gross motor coordination of the lower extremities and balance.

Touching Body Parts

Instruct participants who can maintain standing balance with only one-hand support (or no support) to touch various body parts with the right hand, then the left hand. This maneuver involves crossing the midline of the body, trunk rotation, weight shift, and upper-extremity ROM.

Resistive Exercises

Make any of the foregoing exercises more difficult with cuff weights around the wrists or ankles.

Pulling and Pushing

Another resistive exercise is to tie a 25-foot cord to a chair, walker, or other object, and have the person pull it toward her (Figure 2–22). This is an excellent activity for weight shifting of the lower extremities and trunk rotation; it is a resistive exercise for the upper extremities and abdominal muscles. Pushing a chair or other object across the floor strengthens plantar flexors, knee and hip extensors, and back extensors. With all resistive exercises, one should exhale with the effort; in other words, "don't hold your breath." Avoid the Valsalva maneuver, because it increases intra-abdominal pressure and raises blood pressure.[2,3]

STRETCHING EXERCISES

Cartilage, tendons, and ligaments become stiffer and more rigid with age. Thus they are more prone to injury from sudden stress.[3]

General Guidelines for Teaching Flexibility[4]
1. Start in a comfortable position
2. Move slowly to the end of the range
3. Hold at the end range for 10 to 20 seconds
4. Feel a gentle pull or stretch but no joint pain
5. Return slowly to the starting position

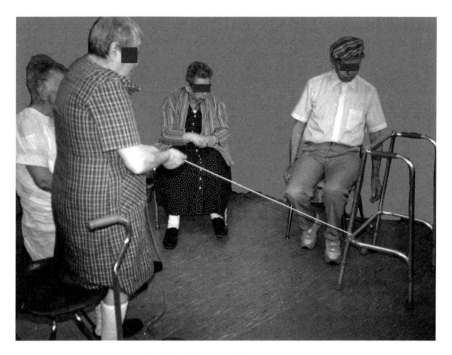

Figure 2–22 The patient pulls the walker toward her.

6. Use slow, coordinated active movement
7. Repeat three to five times

Suggested Stretches[4]

1. Shoulder ROM, shoulder retraction, upper trunk extension, and pectoral stretch using combination movements with a small towel (Figure 2–23).

2. Hamstring stretches. In a sitting position, or standing with support, elevate a foot on a stool with the knee in extension. Reach forward toward the foot (Figure 2–24).

3. Hip flexors. While standing, put one foot behind the other, using a chair for support. Shift center of gravity forward until a gentle stretch is felt at the top of the thigh of the back leg.

4. Trunk rotation and side-bending. With pelvis stabilized, turn upper trunk slowly to the right, then to the left. Lean to one side, approximating ribs and pelvis on that side; then to opposite side.

Shoulders, hamstrings, hip flexors, and trunk muscles often become tight with prolonged sitting. These stretches benefit posture. Except for the hip flexor stretch, these exercises can be done either sitting or standing.

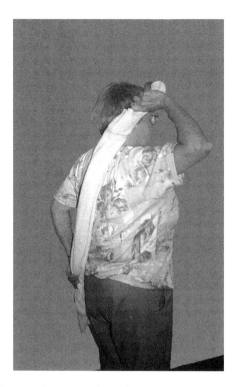

Figure 2–23 Shoulder retraction–pectoral stretch.

VIDEOTAPING

Videotaping each person's transfers and ambulation can be an effective tool for teaching members of the group and the staff. A commercial video-tape demonstrating various transfers and ambulation techniques is not nearly as effective as one you produce yourself, which highlights each patient's strengths and weaknesses. People enjoy seeing themselves on tape and a picture is worth a thousand words. To the group members, offer gentle advice and suggestions on how to improve transfers and gait.

A videotape can also be very useful for staff in-service training. Often aides are surprised to see a patient arise from a chair with only a verbal cue—they may be accustomed to lifting him up. The tape also lets you show the evening and night shifts what each person can do and demonstrates safe techniques for guarding him.

PROGRAM PLANNING FOR A GROUP
OF AMBULATORY PATIENTS

The primary goal for ambulatory patients is reinforcement of safe transfers and gait. Therefore, begin with an activity such as trading chairs, an

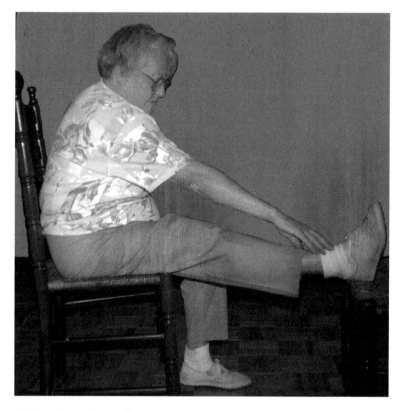

Figure 2–24 Hamstring stretch.

obstacle course, or carrying an object across the circle. Move on to ROM, strengthening exercises, and stretching. Walking longer distances from the exercise area to the patient's room or nursing unit helps improve endurance.

The exercise prescription must be appropriate for both cognitive and physical abilities. Activities that are very simple are boring to a highly functioning group, but the same exercises may be challenging and interesting to another group.

Talk to nursing staff frequently and let them know of the patients' goals and progress. Also involve the family of the patient as often as possible. Family members may be reluctant to take the person home for a day or a weekend because of concerns about safety and mobility or unfamiliarity with the person's needs and routine. Talk with the family and problem-solve about possible barriers, such as steps and doorways, bathroom transfers (toilet and tub or shower), and dressing.

CASE REPORTS

Norwood B

The following case report illustrates how a patient is assisted to maintain transfer skills.

Norwood is 80 years of age. He is a widower who formerly worked in a mushroom plant. He has been hospitalized since he was 65 years of age for dementia secondary to syphilis. Norwood has a history of assaultive behavior and knocking over furniture. For the past 5 years, Norwood's medical problems have increased; now they preclude most of his violent behavior. Norwood has Parkinson's disease, a seizure disorder, atherosclerotic heart disease, tardive dyskinesia, and glaucoma. He is obese, mute, almost blind, and incontinent of bowel and bladder. He has been a resident in long-term care for 3 years.

Norwood has been referred for physical therapy after 6 weeks of gait unsteadiness, which culminated in a fall with facial fractures. At evaluation, Norwood was fairly cooperative and followed simple commands (eg, "get up"), requiring physical and verbal cues to do so. Norwood has a large, stocky build. He has bilateral pes planus, left wrist flexion limited to 20 degrees, and bilateral knee flexion contractures of 30 degrees. Strength could not be tested because Norwood could not follow the directions. He was tactilely defensive with a gross resting tremor of his hands, which he generally kept loosely held together.

Norwood could transfer from sitting to standing with contact guarding. He tended to rock forward and back five to six times before standing up. Transferring from standing to sitting, Norwood moved abruptly, throwing himself into the chair, usually landing on the front edge of the seat. He could walk 50 feet, with close contact guarding, hips and knees flexed, hips widely abducted with a waddling gait and short shuffling steps.

Norwood could participate in activities for the ambulatory group with some adaptations. He could throw a ball in a sitting position with some accuracy if the facilitator called or clapped to help him locate where to throw it. He could not catch a ball but could find it in his lap, and he could pick up a small object from the floor. Physical cues were more effective than verbal instruction or demonstration.

Norwood had many compulsive habits. Despite his very poor vision and his balance problems, he would find a chair and insist on pushing it up to a table or move a trash can. He would also spot a doorknob and insist on turning it. He would become upset with attempts to redirect him from these activities, and would sometimes take a swing at people. This was more dangerous for him than for his caregivers, because of his balance dysfunction.

Because of his severe visual deficits and long-standing balance and gait dysfunction, the therapist could not reasonably expect that Norwood would become independent with ambulation or transfers. He was becoming more of a management problem on the unit for transfers. The therapist decided to include him in an ambulatory exercise group to maintain his ability to transfer and walk with contact guarding.

Norwood was generally cooperative, although he did have difficulty with directions, because of his cognitive deficits. After 3 months, Norwood became ill with upper respiratory and urinary tract infections. He began to have more difficulty with ambulation, experiencing more unsteadiness and increased knee-hip flexion. He could walk only about 20 feet safely. He sometimes required minimal assistance for transfers.

The therapist continued to work with Norwood in the group but pushed him in a chair instead of walking with him from the unit. Norwood then was hospitalized for 2 weeks because of intestinal obstruction. On return from the hospital, the therapist found Norwood needed moderate assistance for transfers and could walk only about 5 feet, with his hips and knees flexed 45 degrees.

Norwood was too unsteady, and too big, to walk safely in the group, even with close contact guarding. He also continued to insist on his rituals; he would dive for a chair and would become angry and take a swing at those who attempted to direct him. The therapist decided to take Norwood to the physical therapy department for ambulation in the parallel bars twice a week. He still preferred to walk with his hands loosely clasped in front of him. He put his hands on the bars when cued and walked two to three times in the bars. Norwood also cooperated in upper-extremity exercises, and the therapist continued to encourage him to use his hands in a group sitting class.

Norwood continued this regimen for 2 months and gradually became stronger. He has returned to the ambulatory group and is doing well, although he can walk only about 20 feet safely. Norwood is marginal with his ambulation, and he will probably continue to experience occasional declines and improvements, depending on his medical problems. Because of his size and inability to follow directions, he would become a severe management problem for nursing if he were to become dependent for transfers. The goal of therapy is to maintain Norwood at his present level for his own sake and to prevent staff injuries.

Lela K

The following patient requires frequent reinforcement of safety instructions and is responding well to exercises in a group.

Lela is 68 years of age, and has a history of psychiatric problems since her early 20's, including delusions and auditory hallucinations. She has been hospitalized with a diagnosis of chronic paranoid schizophrenia. Brief periods of community living with her two sisters have not proved successful. Lela's medical condition includes seizure disorder, chronic obstructive pulmonary disease, mild mental retardation, scoliosis, and previous fractures of the left pelvis and right humerus. She was reportedly independent with transfers and ambulation without an assistive device until 6 months ago. The staff noticed that Lela was unsteady walking, and they attributed the unsteadiness to Lela's agitation and confusion.

Three months after the staff noticed the unsteadiness, Lela was hospitalized for 1 week with dehydration, urinary tract infection, chronic obstructive pulmonary disease, and seizure disorder. At discharge, she was referred to physical therapy for ambulation training.

At evaluation, Lela was largely nonverbal and did not respond to to questions. She sometimes said "Oh God!" in a loud voice or mumbled unintelligibly. Lela had dorsal kyphosis and moderate right thoracolumbar scoliosis. This resulted in a functional, though not actual, leg length discrepancy, with a shortened left leg secondary to an elevated left pelvis. There were arthritic deformities of both hands; ROM was otherwise full. Muscle strength could not be formally tested because of her cognitive deficits, but it appeared within normal limits for Lela's age.

Transfers required moderate assistance of one to the parallel bars or walker. Standing, Lela tended to lean backward. She was unable to maintain standing without support but required both hands on the bars or walker. Using a wheeled walker, Lela pushed it too far ahead and seemed unable to figure out how to get her feet up to the walker. It seemed that Lela could not decide what to do when approaching a chair. She put her knee on the chair, or on seeing a chair, attempted to sit down wherever she was. She seemed to believe the chair would materialize behind her. Lela was not uncooperative but did not appear to comprehend and was unable to follow verbal commands. She also showed decreased motor planning skills and balance.

Lela was seen only three times. Her psychiatric symptoms worsened to psychogenic anorexia and subsequent hyponatremia and dehydration. She was hospitalized for 1 week and on her return was referred again for physical therapy. A nasogastric tube and Foley catheter were in place. Both were discontinued in 1 week. Lela had lost weight and was much weaker than before. Standing pivot transfers required moderate assistance of two. Lela was unable to walk.

Lela received individual physical therapy 22 times in 6 weeks. She was reassessed and showed substantial improvement. Lela continued to respond more to internal stimuli but would sometimes follow verbal and physical cues. She could not be tested on the functional reach (FR) test or Mobility Performance Scale (MPS) (see Chapter 8) because of her cognitive deficits. She could transfer from sitting to standing with close supervision.

The therapist found it necessary to avoid touching Lela before and during transfers, because she would expect to be lifted and would not exert effort. When the walker was stabilized during transfers, Lela would pull up on it. When the therapist did not stabilize the walker, Lela would correctly lean forward and push up from the chair. Transfers from standing to sitting continued to be difficult. Lela could not consistently follow verbal or physical cues to position herself in front of the chair and back up but instead would try to sit down next to, but not in, the chair. She no longer put her knee on the chair.

Because of her cognitive deficits and poor motor planning, Lela could not become independent with transfers and ambulation or progress safely to using a cane. In the nursing unit, Lela fully reclines in a geriatric chair with a tray—to which she often objects. However, sitting up and without the tray, Lela is not reliable in calling for assistance when she wants to get up. Lela had reached a plateau as far as progress in therapy is concerned. She has begun to participate in a group exercise program to maintain her functional status in transfers, ambulation, ROM, strength, and endurance.

Lela has cooperated well with the exercises for the past 6 weeks. She enjoys the company of others and responds to a request to walk over to a chair and sit next to Jean—Jean is her friend. Lela's orientation and ability to communicate vary but have generally improved. She says that her back hurts sometimes, but she describes no other symptoms.

Lela has shown gradual improvement in her ability to walk and transfer. She now requires close supervision only from sitting to standing, and verbal and sometimes physical cues to back up safely to a chair while transferring from standing to sitting. She no longer pushes the walker too far ahead of herself when walking. She can now walk with a wheeled walker 20 feet, propelling it without assistance, but with contact guarding and verbal cues to her destination. She does exhibit a functionally shorter left leg during ambulation. She can maintain independent standing balance with one hand support. During knee extension exercises, Lela often lifts both feet together and becomes fascinated with her socks, especially if they are pink. With her feet stuck straight out, she spends several minutes admiring her "pretty legs." About the only thing that upsets Lela is wearing a dark-colored dress or being asked to sit in a dark chair. She thinks dark colors make her invisible.

Lela is meeting the maintenance goals of the group program.

Daisy M

The following patient derives social, emotional, and physical benefits from participation in group exercise.

Daisy is 67 years of age. Two years ago, she was found to have an inoperable but nonmalignant brain tumor just anterior to the thalamus. She has progressive organic brain syndrome, a seizure disorder, and is confused, nonverbal, and disoriented. She was admitted to the long-term care facility 2 years ago.

Daisy had been independent with all ambulation and transfers. She had no history of falls, but her gait was described as stiff-legged. Two months ago, Daisy stopped walking, indicating pain in her left hip. Radiographs did not show a fracture but indicated severe arthritis in the left hip. Pending orthopedic studies, Daisy had been restrained in a geriatric chair for 2 weeks before she was referred to physical therapy to resume ambulation.

Daisy would mutter unintelligibly, sometimes angrily, but could give no response to questions. She had left hip flexion to 95 degrees; ROM was otherwise full. Despite this, Daisy had a very unusual gait. She would rapidly weight-shift right to left, with a normal step length on the right but only advancing the left foot even with the right. Her left knee remained locked in extension, with 10 degrees of recurvatum. There was slight circumduction of the left lower extremity during swing and no trunk rotation. She either kept her arms folded across her chest or flung them out widely to the side. Although Daisy could not verbalize pain, she appeared uncomfortable transferring from sitting to standing and would reach for the therapist's hand during transfers. The nurses told the therapist that Daisy's gait was the same as her gait before the onset of her hip pain. The only difference was that Daisy no longer seemed to want to walk.

The therapist obtained clearance from an orthopedic surgeon and began to work with Daisy in a group with five other ambulatory patients. She had considerable difficulty following directions for exercises and seemed to prefer to be left alone. When approached slowly and patiently, however, Daisy would participate in simpler activities. Daisy did not show unsteadiness despite her unusual gait. She soon could tolerate getting up and down six or seven times in a 45-minute period. We suggested to the nurses that after she returned from therapy, Daisy could sit in a regular chair or walk under nursing supervision until lunch. This worked well. In a week, Daisy no longer needed to be restrained in a geriatric chair.

Daisy has returned to the level of independence walking that she had before the onset of hip pain. In 3 weeks, Daisy has become accustomed to the group and seems to enjoy it; she has even begun to smile with certain activities. The nurses note some improvements in her socialization as well. Daisy shows less tendency to isolate herself from others. Daisy is invited to participate in the group exercise program as long as she wants to.

Jean T

The following patient's mobility was retained and she was able to resume regular visits home with her daughter. Her daughter was very supportive of her participation.

Jean has been a resident in long-term care for 5 years and is 74 years of age. She was born of immigrant parents and had 12 siblings. Jean married a career pilot in the Air Force, who retired as a lieutenant colonel. He died 20 years ago. Jean has three daughters and a son, who visit frequently. Her oldest daughter enjoys taking her home for visits most weekends, even though Jean has to walk up six steps to get into the house. Jean has rheumatoid arthritis that affects both hands and especially her right knee.

Until 10 months ago, Jean could walk short distances without an assistive device but with a right genu valgus of 20 degrees and ROM of 25 to 90 degrees. She wore a hinged canvas orthosis on her knee. She was independent with all activities of daily living, including donning and doffing the orthosis.

Then just before Christmas, Jean fell, sustaining a comminuted intertrochanteric fracture of the right femur. She underwent an open reduction internal fixation and was referred to physical therapy for transfer and gait training with toe touch weight-bearing only and exercise.

At initial evaluation, Jean's right hip ROM was 0 to 120 degrees. Her right knee ROM was flexion of 35 to 90 degrees with genu valgus of 20 degrees. Jean required moderate assistance to stand in the parallel bars. There she could maintain standing for only 1 to 2 minutes and was unable to advance either foot. Jean reported pain and dizziness with standing. Jean was scheduled for physical therapy five times a week (although she requested therapy only every other day).

Jean participated in exercise, transfer, and gait training, progressing to a walker. Arthritis in her hands caused Jean some difficulty with weight-bearing through her upper extremities, and she used a platform walker initially. Because of the limitation of toe touch weight-bearing (10 percent only) on the right lower extremity, progress was slow. At the end of January, the orthopedic surgeon advanced weight-bearing to as tolerated, and Jean began to progress faster. She continued to receive individual therapy.

By the end of February, Jean was walking 100 feet with a wheeled walker (without platform) with 70 percent weight-bearing on the right with supervision only. The flexion contracture of the right knee improved with ROM of 25 to 90 degrees. Jean again became independent with dressing, including the knee orthosis. Her standing balance on the right foot was limited only by the pain in her knee.

Jean had not had any visits home with her daughter since the hip fracture and missed those visits a great deal. She was very interested in learning car transfers and ascending and descending steps. Eventually she needed only a railing, quad cane, and supervision on steps. She was very happy to tell her daughter about her progress in these areas, and was soon making weekend visits.

The therapist attempted to progress Jean to ambulation with a quad cane. However, after Jean walked only 5 feet, her knee pain became too severe to continue. In March, Jean was examined by the orthopedic surgeon, who recommended a right total knee replacement. Jean was looking forward to more visits home with the family during the summer and decided to wait until fall.

Jean resumed participation in the group exercise program. She was a cooperative and pleasant participant. However, Jean did not walk at all except during therapy and was completely dependent on the wheelchair for mobility on the unit. She would agree to walk to the dining room for one meal a day but would not do it. Attempts to wean Jean from the wheelchair were unsuccessful.

In August, Jean contracted acute bronchitis, which developed into atelectasis of the left lower lung. This has recently resolved. However, Jean has continued to defer right knee replacement because she is concerned about her lungs and frequent cough. (She continues to smoke.) Jean enjoys the group exercise class and often acts as a helper to other patients.

Jean's functional status has been maintained. She has a FR (see Chapter 8) of 7 inches. This would indicate a four times greater than average risk for falls. Her performance on this test seems limited by her knee pain more than balance dysfunction. Jean scored 2/7 on the MPS (see Chapter 8). If Jean ever does consent to surgical treatment to correct the severe deformity of her right knee, she could probably walk with a cane. She continues to refuse to walk independently, but has maintained her functional status in the group program.

REFERENCES

1. Carr, JH. *Movement science: Foundations for physical therapy in rehabilitation.* Rockville: Aspen, 1987.
2. McKirnan MD, Froelicher VF. General principles of exercise testing. In: Skinner, JS. *Exercise testing and exercise prescription for special cases: Theoretical basis and clinical application,* 2d ed. Philadelphia: Lea & Febiger, 1993, pp. 3–27.
3. Kisner C, Colby LA. *Therapeutic exercise: Foundations and techniques,* 2nd ed. Philadelphia: Davis, 1990.
4. May BJ. Principles of exercise for the elderly. In: Basmajian JV, Wolf SL. *Therapeutic exercise,* 5th ed. Baltimore: Williams & Wilkins, 1990, pp. 279–298.

3

Exercises in a Seated Position: Conventional Chair, Wheelchair, or Geriatric Chair

These exercises and activities are for people who are not ambulatory, although they are also useful for those who are. For the latter group, use them to provide variety and a break from more difficult and tiring activities done in a standing position.

Participants should be sitting in a comfortable, erect position with feet supported on the floor or on footrests. Hips, knees, and ankles all should be at 90 degrees. For someone who sits in a wheelchair or geriatric chair for most of the day, posture in the chair is especially important. For people unable to maintain an erect posture, an appropriate seat cushion or positioning device may be required to prevent deformity or pressure ulcers and to promote comfort.

The environment should be as quiet and nondistracting as possible. The room should be at a comfortable temperature without drafts. Participants sit in a circle 10 to 15 feet in diameter so they can easily see each other and the group leader.

Following is a list of activities for seated patients. The exercises emphasize hand activities, motor coordination, range of motion, strengthening of upper and lower extremities, and trunk mobility.

BILATERAL HAND ACTIVITIES AND MOTOR COORDINATION

1. Passing objects. Pass an object, such as a baton or paper towel tube, around the circle. This activity encourages reaching, reinforces directionality, and stimulates awareness and cognition. Ask each participant to pass the baton from one hand to the other under the knees, behind the neck, around the back, or over the shoulder. Encourage socialization by using names, and

encourage participants to address each other by name. ("Pass the stick to John [or Mr. Jones]"). Always call a person by the name he prefers.

2. Pulling an object on a string. Tie a light object to a string 5 to 6 feet long, and ask the participant to pull it toward herself. Encourage a bilateral hand-over-hand movement. Use heavier objects, such as a walker or chair, to increase the resistance.

3. Donning and doffing a hat, scarf, necklace, or watch. Pass the article around the circle, encouraging the participants to reach for and take the object, put it on, take it off, and pass it to the next participant. This involves multistep commands and bilateral use of the hands. Moving the chairs farther apart requires more lateral flexion and trunk stabilization while reaching. Auditory cues (eg, clapping) may help participants with a visual deficit.

4. Object manipulation. Each participant must have a tray or table. Putting together, taking apart, and constructing with plastic blocks (eg, Legos) facilitates fine motor coordination, problem solving, and color recognition. Other activities include stringing beads, stacking blocks, and clipping clothespins to the edge of a container or fabric.

5. Hit a ball attached to a paddle to facilitate eye-hand coordination.

6. Throwing and catching a ball. A Koosh ball or beanbag, which does not roll, is easiest to handle. If a participant misses, he may be encouraged to reach down to the floor to pick the ball up, with close guarding. Ask participants to throw the ball to each other across the circle, using names to encourage socialization (Figures 3–1 and 3–2).

For a participant with severe visual impairment who cannot catch a ball, keep a tray in place so she can retrieve the ball easily from the tray. If the

Figure 3–1 Participants throwing a ball to each other.

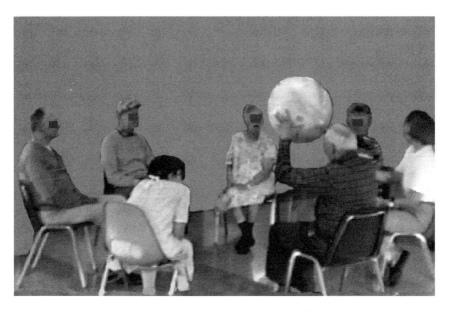

Figure 3–2 Participants throwing a ball to each other (*continued*).

visual impairment prevents the participant from throwing the ball accurately, try auditory cues, such as clapping or calling her name. If a participant still cannot throw accurately enough, tie a string around a soft foam ball so you can retrieve the ball quickly. Participants with good coordination and vision can use a soft inflatable ball 12 inches in diameter to throw or bounce pass across the circle (Figure 3–3).

7. Kicking a ball. Swing away the footrests on wheelchairs. Place the chairs close enough together, or place walkers or chairs between participants, so the ball does not escape the circle.

8. Dribbling a ball. Patients with good coordination may dribble a ball between their feet, an activity for eye-hand coordination and gross motor skills (Figure 3–4).

Ball activities require arousal and prolonged concentration. These are effective initial activities to arouse lethargic participants.

9. Rapid alternating movement (RAM). RAM may be done either in reciprocal or simultaneous patterns. Begin with a 2- to 3-second time interval and gradually increase the speed.

Upper-extremity RAM
Fist open-close
Wrist flexion-extension
Elbow flexion-extension
Supination-pronation
Shoulder flexion-extension
Shoulder elevation-depression.

Figure 3–3 Bouncing a ball to a participant.

Figure 3–4 Dribbling the ball between the knees.

Lower-extremity RAM
Knee extension-flexion
Ankle dorsiflexion—plantar flexion
Hip flexion-extension

10. Grab bag. An assortment of objects is placed in a bag. Ask patients to pull out articles one at a time and explain or demonstrate their use. Good items are a comb, sunglasses, nail file, razor without blade, mirror, gloves, wristwatch or clock, paper and pencil, clothes brush, dental floss, bar of soap, coins, dollar bill, can opener or other kitchen utensils, and tools. This activity facilitates fine motor coordination and stimulates cognition.

11. Parachute activities. Real parachutes can be purchased for outdoor games that involve large numbers of able-bodied people. For indoors, with a group of six to eight seated patients, a flat sheet from a double bed works and is an inexpensive alternative (Figure 3–5). With everyone grasping the sheet in both hands, lift it up high to look underneath it at others across the circle (Figure 3–6). Hold for a count of ten. This activity strengthens the shoulder by requiring co-contraction of the muscles of the shoulder girdle while maintaining sitting balance.

Holding the sheet, rotate it in one direction and then the other. Pin or ask a participant to pin an object to the sheet, and rotate it to the participant across the circle (Figure 3–7). This activity involves motor planning, grasp and release, and fine motor coordination.

With everyone grasping the sheet with both hands, toss a small stuffed pillow or toy on the sheet and ask the group to bounce it around. Many participants enjoy this, and continue the activity long enough to elevate the

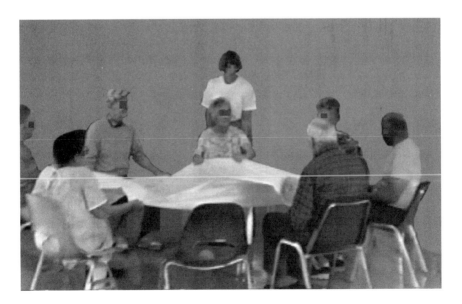

Figure 3–5 Participants are encouraged to grasp the sheet with both hands.

Figure 3–6 Participants hold the sheet high to look underneath it.

Figure 3–7 The sheet is rotated by grasp-release of both hands.

heart rate and enhance cardiopulmonary fitness.[1] It also requires synchronous movements of everyone in the group.

Toss a sheet or pillow case over a person's head and ask him to lift it off. Be very careful to avoid frightening anyone; explain what you are doing before you do it. State the goal as getting the cloth off the person's head as quickly as possible. This activity involves motor planning and upper-extremity range of motion.

For ambulatory patients with very good balance, any of these activities can be done in a standing position.

12. Breaking bubbles. Wave the wand or blow bubbles above a participant's head, and ask her to break them by clapping her hands together or poking the bubbles as they float down. Be careful not to get soap bubbles in anyone's eyes. If the floor is tile, put a towel down to prevent slipping. This is an excellent activity for eye-hand coordination. It can also be done standing. You can use a fan to make the bubbles—lots of them.

ACTIVE RANGE OF MOTION EXERCISES

1. The cervical exercises described in Chapter 2 may be done with eyes open and then closed. Scapular exercises to improve posture may be done in a sitting position.

2. "Look behind." Walk around the outside of the circle and encourage participants to watch you. Or have a participant walk, or wheel himself, around the outside of the circle. This exercise facilitates cervical rotation, which helps in standing-to-sitting transfers and many other activities.

3. Trunk exercises. Ask participants to hold on to the edge of the chair or armrest with one hand and then reach toward the floor on the other side with the opposite hand. Participants can reach with both hands to the floor between their feet, to the left foot with the right hand, and vice versa. These exercises facilitate trunk rotation, lateral flexion, and sitting balance. Functional activities such as pulling up socks and tying shoes or picking up an object from the floor in front or on either side may be incorporated. Carefully guard people who have difficulty with sitting balance.

4. Lower extremity exercises. Tapping toes or heels on the floor facilitates ankle range of motion (ROM). Foot stomping facilitates proprioceptive input through the lower extremities. Knee extension with cues to hold for 3 to 5 seconds strengthen the quadriceps muscle. Cue hip flexion with the knee flexed to strengthen the iliopsoas and rectus femoris muscles. Many patients have weak hip flexors and may need to use the upper extremities to help, either by locking their fingers just below the knee or under the thigh. Crossing and uncrossing the legs also strengthens hip flexion. Combine this exercise with ankle ROM of the top leg. Cue for right or left to strengthen concepts of laterality.

5. Upper extremity ROM. Ask patients to reach down to the floor, then touch feet, knees, hips, shoulders, and head in sequence and finally reach straight up to the ceiling.

Have participants execute elbow flexion and extension with the arms at the sides or at 90 degrees of shoulder flexion-abduction.

Ask patients to place their arms in chicken-wing position and pull their elbows together in back.

Teach wrist flexion-extension and rotation, finger ROM, and clapping. Unilateral reaching to identify body parts, such as elbow, neck, hip, and ankles, encourages concepts of body parts and laterality. Participants with a weak upper extremity because of stroke or injury can lace their fingers together and lift the arms in a frontal or diagonal plane by using the stronger arm to help the motion.

6. Visualization. Visualization requires no equipment, can be done with large or small groups, incorporates full ROM in both upper and lower extremities and the trunk, and is fun. Invite patients to pretend to go on an outing or play a game with you. They may close their eyes to set the mood, but this is not necessary. Some suggestions include the following

A Trip to the Pool
Diving in—bilateral shoulder flexion
Splashing—upper extremity ROM
Bobbing underwater, blowing bubbles—breath control
Swimming strokes (crawl, breast, side, back)—full shoulder and elbow ROM
Floating on back or stomach, rotary breathing—cervical ROM in all planes
Climbing up ladder out of pool or on diving ladder—reciprocal upper- and lower-extremity movement
Drying off with towel reaching for all parts of the body, including feet and behind the back—trunk flexion, extension, rotation

A Basketball Game
Dribbling the ball between the feet with one or two hands—reciprocal movement
Passing the ball to the side, bouncing or throwing—trunk rotation
Shooting one- or two-handed, set, hook, slam dunk—upper extremity ROM
Faking right, left—trunk rotation, lateral flexion
Referee signals

A Hike in the Woods
Putting on boots, equipment—trunk ROM
Putting on insect repellent, sun block—upper extremity ROM, use of hands
Walking, high stepping—hip flexion
Looking for birds (use a bird whistle for added realism)—cervical ROM
Smelling flowers or a skunk—diaphragmatic breathing

A Fishing Trip
Paddling the rowboat—shoulder ROM, synchronized movement
Rocking, tipping the boat—trunk lateral flexion, protective reactions
Dropping anchor—bilateral hand-over-hand movement
Casting the rod, pulling in a fish—upper extremity ROM

You can play almost any sport, game, or activity in the imagination with opportunities for exercise and fun. Other ideas include baseball, deep sea diving, and skiing. Conducting an orchestra, picking apples, chopping or sawing wood, and playing a musical instrument are good hand and upper-extremity activities.

STRENGTHENING EXERCISES

Resistive Exercises

Cuff weights placed on wrists or ankles for the active ROM exercises described earlier increase the difficulty. Sitting push-ups strengthen shoulder depressors and elbow extensor muscles. Theraband or Theratubing come in six graded resistances to accommodate various abilities. A somewhat less expensive alternative is surgical tubing. Cut either in 3-foot lengths.

Upper Extremity Exercises Tie the ends of the band together and loop around the push handle of the wheelchair. Have the participant place his hand in the loop and push out, protracting the shoulder and extending the elbow. Put the tubing through the top of the footrests or the lower part of the armrest with the loop in the hand for resisted elbow flexion and shoulder internal rotation (on the same side) or shoulder external rotation (opposite side).

Lower Extremity Exercises Loop the tubing from the wheelchair frame around the ankle for resisted knee extension. Have the person hold the ends with the tubing under the forefoot for resisted plantar flexion.

Isometric Exercises

Ask the participants to squeeze a foam ball in one hand to strengthen grip or between the palms of both hands to strengthen wrist flexion and shoulder adduction. Encourage her to hold the contraction for a 5- to 10-second count.

Balloon Activities

Blowing up a balloon, releasing the air, and tying it closed require fine motor coordination. For isometric exercise, have participants squeeze the balloon between the knees (hip adductors), between the palms of the hands (wrist flexors), or under the arms (shoulder adduction). Lift the balloon up overhead, then down to the floor. Bat it overhead. Roll the balloon under the feet to facilitate proprioception and somatosensory input to the lower extremities.

Hugs

Ask everyone to give themselves a hug now and then. This is an isometric exercise for the upper extremities and muscles of the shoulder girdle.

STRETCHING EXERCISES

Stretching exercises are described in Chapter 2. All except the hip flexor stretch can be done by a seated patient. Patients unable to stand have difficulty stretching the hip flexors. Probably the most effective stretch is prone positioning; however, many older people are unable to tolerate lying prone. An alternative is side-lying on a mat or bed. All stretches can be done actively if the participant is able or passively by the facilitator if the patient is not able.

WHEELCHAIR POSITIONING

Any participant who is not a functional ambulator should be seated in an appropriate wheelchair. Depending on trunk strength, with positioning inserts as necessary, the patient should sit as erect as possible. The ideal position is with hips, knees, and ankles all at 90 degrees. Adjust footrests to the correct length so hips and knees are at 90 degrees. Sometimes footrests are removed from wheelchairs—the nurse may forget to put them back on after a transfer or may be encouraging the patient to push the chair with his forefeet. Unfortunately, in this position the ankles are plantar flexed, which can lead to contractures. The weight of the person's thighs can cause an anterior pelvic tilt and an increase in lumbar lordosis, which may cause back pain. Or she may slide forward in the chair, resulting in sacral sitting and risk of pressure ulcers.

A wheelchair that is appropriate and properly adjusted encourages alertness and interaction with the environment, prevents contractures, and promotes use of the hands for activities of daily living. Wheelchair fittings should be performed by an experienced physical or occupational therapist and the medical equipment supplier, who is familiar with the type of equipment available. Possible adaptations include a reclined back, removable armrests, swing-away removable leg rests, and elevating leg rests.

The patient may need a customized seating system with foam or gel inserts to position his trunk and prevent joint contractures. For patients at risk for pressure ulcers, an air, foam, or gel seat cushion combined with weight shifts[2] (independently or assisted by staff) every 15 to 30 minutes is recommended.

Whenever possible, the participant should learn to propel and maneuver the wheelchair herself. If the patient lacks sufficient upper-extremity strength or ROM to operate a manual chair but is cognitively intact, a motorized wheelchair allows the greatest degree of independent mobility.

GERIATRIC CHAIRS

Reclining chairs, often called geriatric chairs, should be avoided whenever possible. They place the patient in a position of dependence for all mobility. The person is unable to use the hands for most functional activities.

When the patient is reclined, ankles are plantar flexed, knees are flexed about 25 degrees, and hips are flexed 45 to 60 degrees. The person is at risk for contractures, especially of the ankles and hips. This is true even in the absence of spasticity. If the patient has had a stroke or has any other neurologic condition that causes an increase in tone, contractures are even more likely to occur.

Geriatric chairs with trays are often used as a covert form of restraint. They are used for patients who may have a psychiatric or cognitive impairment and are likely to try to get up without supervision, which poses a safety risk to themselves or others. A geriatric chair with tray may appear to be less restraining than a wheelchair with lap belt, but it is not. Even a geriatric chair without a tray, when completely reclined, restrains a patient.

Geriatric chairs are impossible to get out of, even for an able-bodied person, except by rolling out the side onto the floor. As previously discussed, an appropriately fitted wheelchair correctly and comfortably positions a patient and allows for functional mobility. A geriatric chair does not.

A geriatric chair should be used only after careful evaluation and if it has been determined that the patient absolutely cannot use a wheelchair. For example, a person with severe ballistic movement, as may occur with Huntington's disease, can actually tip over a wheelchair.

WHEELCHAIR MOBILITY

People who use wheelchairs for mobility need to learn to propel and maneuver them and operate brakes, swing away leg rests, removable leg rests, and arm rests. Users should be able to retrieve an object from the floor, either by leaning over to pick it up or by using a reacher. They should be able to relieve buttock pressure by executing a sitting push-up or weight shift. These activities can be taught and reinforced in a group exercise class. Races, follow-the-leader games, obstacle courses, and scavenger hunts are but a few ways to develop wheelchair skills. Noting the time required to traverse a course or to "parallel park" reinforces patients' efforts and provides an objective measurement of progress.

VIDEOTAPING

Wheelchair skills can be reinforced with the use of a videotape. Patients enjoy watching themselves on tape. A staff in-service training session promoting independent mobility among wheelchair users can be effective in helping carry-over of skills on other shifts and weekends. Staff members often are surprised to see a tape of a patient propelling his wheelchair independently. A simple change in routine, such as a patient's pushing herself to the dining room for meals instead of being pushed by staff, encourages independence and autonomy.

PROGRAM PLANNING FOR A GROUP OF NONAMBULATORY PATIENTS

Begin with an activity to arouse and interest participants, such as throwing a ball or passing objects around the circle. Then move on to ROM, coordination, resistive exercise, and stretching. The exercise prescription for wheelchair users should include strengthening of mobility and management skills. Independence in wheelchair mobility can be reinforced by cueing patients as needed to push and maneuver the wheelchairs back to the nursing unit.

CASE REPORTS

The following two patients are participating in group sitting exercises and therapeutic standing and ambulation. James L is also reinforced in wheelchair skills and mobility.

James L

James is 81 years of age, never married; he has a niece in a nearby state who maintains contact through the social services department. He has been a resident of a long-term care facility for 8 years. James's medical diagnoses are primary degenerative dementia, arthritis of the knees, and a history of tuberculosis and syphilis, which were treated. He has not been ambulatory for about 5 years. James was referred for physical therapy evaluation.

At evaluation, James spoke in short phrases. He offered to shake hands but then painfully squeezed the therapist's hand. Sometimes James would say, "Don't kill me." He actively resisted ROM testing and tried to hit the therapist. James was fully reclined in a geriatric chair, and because his caregivers remained alert, James was not able to connect with these swings. His upper extremity ROM was tested functionally, by having him reach for an object, which he then refused to return. Upper extremity ROM was within functional limits. In the geriatric chair, James leaned 30 degrees to the right side and resisted attempts to reposition him in the chair. Lower extremity ROM was knee flexion 25 to 90 degrees, plantar flexion 10 to 60 degrees, and hip flexion to 60 degrees. James had an increase in muscle tone throughout. He was quite rigid, especially in the trunk and lower extremities. Nevertheless, when James was asked if he would like to walk, he said yes.

James's functioning was evaluated in the parallel bars. James required moderate assistance of two to come to standing in the bars, due to the tightness in the hip extensors from years in the geriatric chair. With hip flexion to 60 degrees only, James achieved standing only by leaning back and simultaneously pulling up with both hands on the parallel bars. He did walk in the bars with very short steps, with hips and knees flexed 30 degrees, and weight-bearing with left foot flat and on the right forefoot. James required continuous encouragement and some assistance to advance his hands on the bars and to turn around in the bars. James could walk 8 feet twice, resting for 10 minutes after each time.

James participated in a sitting group exercise program five times a week and stood and walked in the parallel bars twice a week. Maintenance goals included preserving strength and ROM and also standing to facilitate transfers on the nursing unit. James enjoyed the exercises, including passing and manipulating objects and resistive exercises using a Theraband. He especially enjoyed throwing and catching a ball and hitting a ball suspended on a string with a bat. He could walk in the parallel bars with some assistance, but his contractures and rigidity prevented him from advancing to a walker.

James would never be a functional ambulator. But he was usually awake and alert. Slumped to the right side in the geriatric chair, he was completely dependent on others for mobility. Perhaps if he had some independent mobility, James might become less aggressive and hostile.

The therapist began working with James in a wheelchair with a reclined back, removable armrests, swing-away elevating leg rests and antitip wheels. Because of the hip contractures, the back was reclined 30 degrees; otherwise James's buttocks would slide forward and his feet would slide off the footrests. In cooperation with the nurses, the therapist gradually increased the time James spent in the chair each day. The staff was at first apprehensive concerning transfers and was instructed on how to help James by having him pull to stand using a hall railing in front of him. He could then stand long enough to put the wheelchair behind him.

The therapist noticed that some staff would remove the footrests for transfers, but then would not put them back on. James tended to push strongly with his feet on the floor, which threatened to tip the chair backward, despite the antitip feature. Sometimes a staff member would try to raise the back to 90 degrees, believing that James would then sit up straighter. As mentioned, this would only cause his buttocks to slide forward and his feet to slide off the footrests (Figure 3–8 and 3–9).

It required many discussions with the staff on how to operate the swing-away footrests for transfers and how to replace them and on the importance of the back being reclined. Eventually everyone was operating the chair consistently. James's posture improved in the wheelchair; he no longer leaned to the side and he stayed awake for longer periods during the day.

The therapist began to work with James on propelling and maneuvering the wheelchair himself. He can propel the chair 50 feet and maneuver through doorways with cues and encouragement only. Sometimes he asks to be carried or bangs on the side of the chair. The therapist made a videotape of James walking in the parallel bars and pushing his chair independently. Many staff members were surprised to see how much James could do for himself, and they have begun to encourage him to push the wheelchair himself. James's ROM has improved in his ankles (to neutral) probably because of better positioning of his feet on the footrests and the ambulation in the

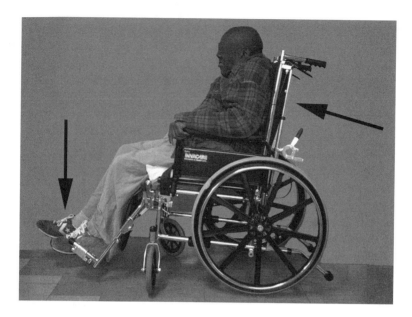

Figure 3–8 The wheelchair back is at 90 degrees to the seat; however, the patient's buttocks are forward in the chair; his feet have slid off the footrests (arrow); and with his forearms on the armrests, his shoulders are elevated (arrow).

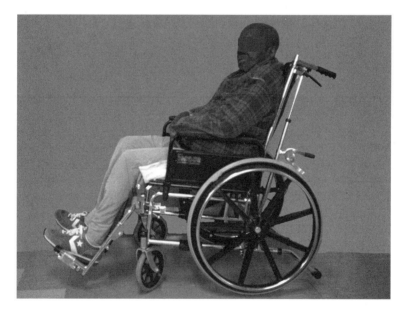

Figure 3–9 With the wheelchair back reclined 15 degrees, the patient is well back in the seat, his thighs and feet are supported, and his shoulders are in a relaxed, natural position.

parallel bars. Hip flexion is now 75 degrees, and James can tolerate the chair reclined just 15 degrees from vertical. Knee flexion is unchanged at 25 to 90 degrees.

James was hospitalized during the summer with syncope and a urinary tract infection. He returned without a noticeable physical decline, but there were reports that he "punched out" a nurse at the hospital. He continues to exhibit aggressive behavior and sometimes tries to hit people walking past him. James's temperament has not improved since he began using the wheelchair for mobility. He does, however, continue to participate in a sitting exercise program, walk in the parallel bars, and receive reinforcement of his wheelchair skills. Maintenance goals are being met.

Thomas G

Thomas is 62 years of age. He is a high school graduate and was employed until 1985. He is divorced and has two sons. At the age of 47 years, Thomas began to exhibit the symptoms of Huntington's disease (his father and uncle died of the disease). The uncoordinated movements and mood swings typical of Huntington's disease made it impossible for Thomas's sons to care for him at home.

Thomas was admitted to a nursing home 6 years ago. He remained ambulatory there; however, he became assaultive to other patients and staff. Two years later, he was admitted to a state psychiatric hospital.

At the psychiatric hospital, Thomas's physical symptoms worsened. After he was there for 6 months he fell, fracturing his left hip, and underwent a bipolar hip replacement. Over the next year, Thomas also gradually lost the ability to speak, to dress, or to feed himself. He required total care for activities of daily living. Thomas was again admitted to a long-term care facility 1 year ago and referred to physical therapy for evaluation of his functioning.

Thomas was nonverbal, although he could understand and follow simple one-step commands, such as "touch your head." Predominant were almost continuous involuntary movements of his extremities and writhing movements that included his trunk. Thomas was reclined in a geriatric chair. At 6 feet 1 inch tall, he could not tolerate a wheelchair unless his trunk and extremities were restrained. From the geriatric chair, Thomas could throw and catch a ball with surprising accuracy, reach and pick up objects from the floor with his long arms, touch body parts on command, and pass and manipulate objects with some difficulty. He could sit at bedside unsupported for several minutes. In the geriatric chair, Thomas had difficulty maintaining his trunk in alignment and was often slumped to the right side. At initial evaluation, Thomas did not have any shoes or slippers, so standing and walking could not be evaluated. With the help of the social worker, shoes were obtained for Thomas about 2 weeks later.

The therapist found that Thomas could stand with moderate assistance of one person. He could walk with a wheeled walker 50 feet, with contact guard of two. He would maintain both elbows in full extension, with about 50 percent of weight-bearing through his upper extremities. He exhibited severe choreoathetoid movements of his lower extremities during gait.

The therapist decided to place Thomas in a sitting group exercise program for ROM and strengthening exercises. He also works on ambulation with the walker twice a week. Goals are to maintain his functional ability as much as possible, taking into account the progressive nature of his disease. He has been generally cooperative. In the last 3 months Thomas has had a gradual increase in his choreoathetoid movements. He now requires assistance to advance the walker and continuous balance assistance to maintain standing.

Thomas has continued to cooperate with the group exercises for the last 6 months. He enjoys throwing and catching a ball, he can pass and manipulate an object, and follows instructions for active exercises. He continues to walk short distances with some assistance. Thomas participates and obviously enjoys the activities. The goals of therapy are being met.

SUPPLIERS

Koosh Ball
ODDz On Products, Inc.
Campbell, CA 95009.
1-408-379-3906
Available in toy stores

Parachute
Sportime Abilitation
1 Sportime Way
Atlanta, GA 30340
1-800-283-5700

Parachute
Gym Closet
2511 Leach Road
Rochester Hills, MI 48309
1-800-445-8873

Parachute
Smith and Nephew Rolyan
P.O. Box 555
Menomonee Falls, WI 53052-0555
1-800-558-8633

Theraband, Theratubing
The Hygenic Corporation
1245 Home Avenue
Akron, OH 44310-2575
1-800-321-2135
Available through many medical and physical therapy supply catalogues

REFERENCES

1. American College of Sports Medicine. *Guidelines for exercise testing and prescription.* 4th ed. Philadelphia: Lea & Febiger, 1991.
2. Lewis CB. *Improving mobility in older persons: A manual for geriatric specialists.* Gaithersburg: Aspen, 1989.

4

Cardiovascular and Pulmonary Conditioning

There are benefits to cardiopulmonary exercise regardless of the person's age. These include conditioning the cardiovascular system, reducing cardiovascular risk, enhancing the fat–to–lean mass ratio, and lowering serum cholesterol levels.[1-9] Even people with cardiac or pulmonary disease or diabetes can benefit from a carefully designed exercise program.[10-15] The exercise prescription for older people must be based on a complete evaluation of the cardiopulmonary and musculoskeletal systems.

AGE-RELATED RESPONSES IN CARDIOPULMONARY SYSTEMS TO EXERCISE

Older people experience a gradual decline in aerobic capacity.[1,3,11] The maximum heart rate decreases with age because of reduction in sympathetic activity and a stiffening of the heart muscle.[3,11] Elderly people are vulnerable to brief episodes of heart failure and possible syncope. The aging cardiovascular and respiratory systems are less capable of adapting than are younger systems. In addition, some medications artificially depress heart rate. Older people can improve their cardiorespiratory health with moderate exercise, but it is necessary to carefully monitor vital signs,[3,11] including heart rate and rhythm and blood pressure.

EXERCISE PRESCRIPTION

Moderate exercise is defined by the American College of Sports Medicine[16] as exercise at an intensity well within the person's current capacity that can be sustained for a prolonged period of time (that is, 60 minutes), is of slow progression, and is generally noncompetitive. Guidelines for safe exercise prescription[16] recommend that apparently healthy people of any age can participate in such a program without the need for stress testing as long as the program begins and proceeds gradually. People of any age with symptoms or signs of cardiopulmonary or metabolic disease, or with known disease, should undergo a medical examination and a physician-supervised test before beginning an exercise program.[16]

Cardiorespiratory fitness improves with exercise that uses large muscle groups and is sustained over 15 to 60 minutes of continuous or discontinuous aerobic activity. The intensity should correspond to 55 to 90 percent of maximal heart rate. (The predicted maximum heart rate is formula 220 minus the person's age.) The frequency of exercise recommended is 3 to 5 days a week.[16]

Exercise of low intensity increases the fitness of some people, especially those who have been inactive. Recent studies[17,18] have demonstrated improvements in functional capacity and activities of daily living even with low-intensity exercise.

HEART RATE

Plan the exercise program for older people to keep the target heart rate at 55 to 90 pecent of the maximum rate calculated from the formula 220 minus age. Thus the heart rate of a 70-year-old person during exercise (maximum predicted rate of 150 beats per minute) should range from 83 to 135 beats per minute. A safe exercise intensity for patients with angina should be 10 beats per minute below the point of ischemic chest pain.[16]

For relatively sedentary people, walking usually increases the heart rate adequately to achieve cardiovascular benefits. The exerciser should walk or exercise at an elevated heart rate for at least 10 minutes. With consistent exercise, a training effect can develop, decreasing the resting and submaximal heart rates.[4-7] In addition, heart rate returns to resting value more quickly after exercise.[7] Recording time required to recover resting heart rate and decreases in resting and submaximal heart rates can provide a measurement of improvement in cardiovascular conditioning.

It is usually not difficult to monitor heart rate at the radial artery at rest and during exercise or ambulation. If the person has severe peripheral vascular disease, and the pulse is not palpable at the wrist, you may need to check the heart rate at the carotid artery. Obtain a baseline for each participant's pulse rate at rest and during the highest level of activity they can sustain for 10 minutes.[19] Before elderly people start exercising, the resting pulse should be 60 to 100 beats per minute and the rhythm should be regular.[3]

BLOOD PRESSURE

Blood pressure rises during exercise but drops within 2 to 3 minutes after exercise stops.[20] It is most accurate to check blood pressure while the person is exercising or immediately afterward. It can be difficult to monitor the blood pressure of a patient who is standing and while guarding him; have someone assist with this.

Obtain a baseline for resting blood pressure. If the resting systolic blood pressure is more than 150 mmHg, the exerciser should proceed with caution. In the elderly, systolic blood pressure more than 160 mmHg or diastolic blood pressure more than 100 mmHg is considered hypertension.[3] Systolic blood pressure normally rises 5 to 10 mmHg within 3 minutes of the beginning of vigorous exercise. Diastolic pressure either falls or remains unchanged from resting.[21] A fall in systolic pressure indicates decompensation and is a reason for terminating exercise. Failure of systolic blood pressure to rise with vigorous exercise also is an abnormal finding.[21]

If a patient has a history of falls or positional vertigo, evaluate for postural hypotension as a cause. Do this by checking blood pressure with the patient supine, sitting, and standing. If a large drop (20 mmHg) in systolic pressure occurs in an upright posture or the patient complains of dizziness, alert the physician of these findings.

Patients who take antihypertensive medications may have difficulty exercising.[22] Diuretics may cause an electrolyte imbalance and blood volume depletion, which reduce blood flow to muscles. Beta-blockers can limit the rise in heart rate and cardiac output. However, even these patients can achieve a training effect.[22] Exercise is especially beneficial for patients with hypertension. There is evidence that resting systolic[4,7] and diastolic[5] blood pressure decreases in the long term with exercise. Even in the short term, blood pressure remains lowered for at least 12 hours after low-intensity to moderate exercise.[22]

PULMONARY FUNCTION

Reinforce deep, diaphragmatic breathing for heart and lung function. The activities that follow may be done in a group or with individual patients. They emphasize expiration, which is taught to last twice as long as inspiration.[23]

1. Blowing a pinwheel or whistle
2. Blowing up balloons, also useful to enhance hand function.
3. Blowing through a straw into a glass of water or to propel a floating object across a water surface
4. Blowing out candles; try the kind that automatically relight
5. Blowing bubbles (Figure 4–1). Either hold the wand, or ask the patients to hold it themselves. Watch for patients who tend to put the wand in their mouths.
6. Have the patients place their hands on the lower rib cage and concentrate on deepening inspiration and lengthening expiration. A 3-second hold at maximal inspiration increases gas diffusion time.[24]

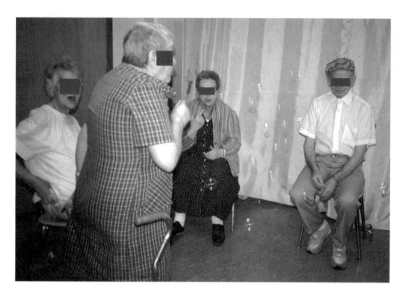

Figure 4–1 Blowing bubbles.

During ambulation and exercise, reinforce diaphragmatic breathing. Emphasize relaxed (not forceful) expiration and avoiding use of upper-chest accessory muscles for inspiration.[23,25] Monitor breathing patterns especially for signs of hyperventilation, anxiety, or breath-holding. The person should be able to talk normally during exercise and ambulation.

Many patients with pulmonary disease often naturally develop or can be taught pursed-lip breathing. The rationale for pursed-lip breathing is unclear and controversial, but many patients do obtain symptomatic relief with this technique.[25] If the patient becomes short of breath, stop the activity and have him take six to eight slow, deep breaths inhaling through the nose and exhaling through pursed lips. Calmly reassure the patient that he is able to stop and rest, that his perceived fatigue is appropriate for the level of exertion, and most important that he can trust your judgment and training. Of course, be sure to report any unusual observations or patient complaints to the nurse or doctor.

WARNING SIGNS DURING EXERCISE

The risk that exercise could precipitate cardiac arrest or ventricular fibrillation is very small. For men 65 to 70 years of age, this risk has been estimated at 1 in 27,000; the risk for elderly women is approximately one-third that for men.[3] Some indicators that circulation is not adequate for the intensity of exercise are as follows[1,3,16]

Decreasing heart rate with increasing activity level
Pain in the chest, arm, or jaw
Irregular heart rate
Excessive dyspnea
Cool and clammy skin
Nausea
Decreased coordination
Confusion
Dizziness
Headache

Instruct patients to inform you immediately if they experience any of these symptoms, and watch for them yourself. With careful monitoring, the benefits of improved cardiovascular health, functional capacity, sleep patterns, and cerebral function seem to outweigh possible risks.[1,26]

CASE REPORT

In the following case report, John F has chronic pulmonary disease with shortness of breath. Side effects of medication also affect his functional ability.

John F

John has been separated from his wife 25 years. He has five daughters. He is a high school graduate and worked at a refinery as a rigger. He has been unable to work for the last 20 years because of poor health and is now 69 years of age.

John's medical history includes organic brain syndrome, upper motor neuron disease secondary to a skull fracture, seizure disorder, chronic obstructive pulmonary disease, and alcoholism. He was admitted to a nursing home 7 years ago but reportedly could not be cared for there because of assaultive behavior and agitation. His daughters say he was mild and loving in nature before his admission, and they suspect he was abused. He was admitted to a psychiatric hospital. John did not exhibit severe behavior problems there and was admitted to the long-term care unit at the psychiatric hospital 3 months later. John was ambulatory at admission to the long-term care unit, but in 5 years his physical condition had deteriorated and he was no longer able to walk.

John is seated in a conventional wheelchair. He is often asleep, but awakens easily. He can transfer from sitting to standing with supervision and cues but tends to look for and expect assistance from a person standing beside him. The therapist finds it is best to stand very close to John during transfers but not to touch him because he then expects physical assistance he does not actually need.

John's standing balance is impaired; he requires both hands on a walker to maintain one-foot standing balance. John also exhibits postural insecurity and fear of falling. He can walk more than 100 feet with a wheeled walker with short shuffling steps and a rigid trunk. He occasionally becomes short of breath. Sometimes he places his right foot outside the walker, but he can be cued to correct. Transferring from standing to sitting, John usually expects to have someone bring a chair up behind him, but he can be cued to turn and back up to the chair safely. John scored 2/7 on the Mobility Performance Scale (MPS) (see Chapter 8). He can propel and maneuver his wheelchair independently, but often expects someone to push him.

John has been functional at this level for the past several months. The staff does not have the time to walk with John. Because of his level of involvement, it is unlikely John can become an independent ambulator. John would benefit from a program to reinforce his ability to transfer and ambulate, and if possible improve his endurance. He participates in a group exercise program, emphasizing transfers, ambulation, coordination, and balance. John has been a willing participant. He is not usually verbal, but sometimes walking back to the unit, he becomes short of breath and says "I'm falling apart, I can't make it!" The therapist then just asks him to stop, take some deep breaths, and note that there are no pieces of him falling off that can be seen. He then smiles and walks farther.

Because of his occasional shortness of breath, the therapist monitors John's heart rate. His resting heart rate was 52 beats per minute and regular. During and after ambulation, heart rate increased to only 60 beats per minute and regular with shortness of breath and returned to 52 beats per minute and regular after 5 minutes of rest. The physician was notified of the low heart rate, and John's regular dose of benzodiazepine, prescribed for anxiety, was decreased. John's resting heart rate increased to 60 beats per minute. During ambulation his heart rate was 96 beats per minute, returning to baseline after 5 minutes of rest.

Three months after John's medication was adjusted the therapist noticed he had become more lethargic. In fact, he seemed about to fall off his chair. This was mentioned to the nurse, who said he had received benzodiazepine a short time previously. The drug was to control his "agitation." John never exhibited agitated behavior in therapy, and the nurse, on reflection, said she had not noticed any agitation recently either. The doctor discontinued the benzodiazepine completely (except before clinic visits or blood tests). Since the drug was discontinued, John has been more alert and better able to participate in exercise. He continues to become short of breath sometimes walking more than 50 feet, but his endurance has generally improved.

REFERENCES

1. Shepard RJ. The scientific basis of exercise prescribing for the very old. *J Am Geriatr Soc* 1990;38:62–70.

2. Lampman RM. Evaluating and prescribing exercise for elderly patients. *Geriatrics* 1987;42:63–65,69–70,73–76.

3. Mount, J. Designing exercise programs for the elderly. In: Rothman JR, Levine R, eds. *Prevention practice: Strategies in physical therapy and occupational therapy.* Philadelphia: Saunders, 1992, pp. 218–233.

4. Amundsen LR, DeVahl JM, Ellingham CT. Evaluation of a group exercise program for elderly women. *Phys Ther* 1989;69:475–483.

5. Koro T. Physical training in the aged person. *Jpn Circ J* 1990;54:1465–1470.

6. Morey MC, Cowper PA, Feussner JR, et al. Evaluation of a supervised exercise program in a geriatric population. *J Am Geriatr Soc* 1989;37:348–354.

7. Steinhaus LA, Dustman RE, Ruhling RO, et al. Aerobic capacity of older adults: A training study. *J Sports Med Phys Fitness* 1990;30:163–172.

8. Levine GN, Balady GJ. The benefits and risks of exercise training: The exercise prescription. *Adv Intern Med* 1993;38:57–79.

9. Judge JO. Exercise programs for older persons: Writing an exercise prescription. *Conn Med* 1993;57:269–275.

10. Coats AJ. Exercise rehabilitation in chronic heart failure. *J Am Coll Cardiol* 1993;22 (Suppl A):172A–177A.

11. Anderson JM. Rehabilitating elderly cardiac patients. *West J Med* 1991;154:573–578.

12. Koch M, Douard H, Broustet JP. The benefit of graded physical exercise in chronic heart failure. *Chest* 1992;101 (Suppl):231S–235S.

13. Carter R, Coast JR, Idell S. Exercise training in patients with chronic obstructive pulmonary disease. *Med Sci Sports Exerc* 1992;24:281–291.

14. Siddigui MA. Cardiac rehabilitation and elderly patients. *Age Ageing* 1992;21:157–159.

15. Maynard T. Exercise. II. Translating the exercise prescription. *Diabetes Educ* 1991;17:384–395.

16. American College of Sports Medicine. *Guidelines for exercise testing and prescription,* 4th ed. Philadelphia: Lea & Febiger, 1991.

17. Brown M, Holloszy JO. Effects of a low intensity exercise program on selected physical performance characteristics of 60- to 71-year olds. *Aging.* 1991;3:129–139.

18. Gorman KM, Posner JD. Benefits of exercise in old age. *Clin Geriatr Med* 1988;4:181–192.

19. Irwin SC, Zadai CC. Cardiopulmonary rehabilitation of the geriatric patient. In Lewis CB, ed. *Aging: The health care challenge,* 2nd ed. Philadelphia: Davis, 1990.

20. Sannerstedt R. Hypertension. In: Skinner JS, ed. *Exercise testing and exercise prescription for special cases: Theoretical basis and clinical application,* 2d ed. Philadelphia: Lea & Febiger, 1993, pp. 275–289.

21. Fletcher GF. *Exercise in the practice of medicine,* 2d ed. Mount Kisco: Futura, 1988.

22. Kaplan NM. The promises and perils of treating the elderly hypertensive. *Am J Med Sci* 1993;305:183–197.

23. Sinclair JD. Exercise in pulmonary disease and disability. In: Basmajian JV, Wolf SL, eds. *Therapeutic exercise,* 5th ed. Baltimore: Williams & Wilkins, 1990, pp. 405–430.

24. Rodrigues JC, Ilowite JS. Pulmonary rehabilitation in the elderly patient. *Clin Chest Med* 1993;14:429–436.

25. Kisner C, Colby LA. *Therapeutic exercise: Foundations and techniques,* 2d ed. Philadelphia: Davis, 1990.

26. Skinner, JS. Importance of aging for exercise testing and exercise prescription. In: Skinner JS, ed. *Exercise testing and exercise prescription for special cases: Theoretical basis and clinical application,* 2d ed. Philadelphia: Lea & Febiger, 1993, pp. 75–86.

5

Shoulder Disability

Various diseases can result in limitations in shoulder strength, range of motion (ROM), and function. Arthritis can cause gradual disuse atrophy. Patients who have undergone mastectomy frequently have pain and limited shoulder ROM. Acute stroke, fractures, and rotator cuff tears, with or without surgical repair, are other common causes. All of these may cause a decrease in ROM, loss of strength, pain with activity, or all three. As a result, the person is no longer able to use the limb for activities of daily living (ADL), especially dressing, bathing, reaching, and other bilateral hand tasks.

An elderly person who has lost function in the lower extremities or back may be further disabled by a shoulder or upper-extremity injury. She must use her upper extremities to assist in pushing up to sitting and in transferring to stand and to use an assistive device. A severe shoulder injury may lead to a permanent loss of self-care and independence.[1]

Many people believe it is fortunate if it is the nondominant shoulder affected. However, the dominant (preferred) hand usually continues to be used for ADL, and use of the arm and at least partial shoulder ROM is thus preserved. The injured nondominant extremity is often ignored, especially after active rehabilitation, and this can result in contractures and weakness of the hand, wrist, and elbow as well as the shoulder. A person who has cognitive or psychiatric dysfunction may be especially reluctant to use the arm.

INDICATIONS FOR A SHOULDER PROGRAM

A maintenance program for shoulder ROM and strength is indicated for those at risk because of the following factors

1. Nonpreferred upper extremity involved
2. Cognitive deficit present
3. Residual disability after a plateau has been reached during rehabilitation
4. Pain at the end of available ROM, which often predicts that the person will not continue full use of the arm, especially if it is nondominant

SUGGESTED EXERCISES

The following exercises and activities are suggested for a group of patients with shoulder disability. Each activity is a station. The participants rotate through the various activities, allowing about 5 minutes for each. Depending on the patients' abilities, they may need physical cues, verbal cues, or assistance, or they may carry out the activity independently.

1. Overhead pulleys (or a cord over a bar) (Figure 5–1)
2. Finger ladder (or tape markers on a wall) (Figure 5–2)
3. Shoulder wheel
4. Pendulum exercises, with or without cuff weight at wrist
5. Clothespins—reaching up to clip the pin to a curtain (Figure 5–3)
6. Thumbtacks—reaching up to push into a bulletin board
7. Hitting or batting at a whiffle or foam ball suspended by a string overhead. Use a foam bat or one made from a short stick and padded with a towel. The higher the suspended ball, the greater is the excursion in shoulder flexion (Figure 5–4).
8. Cane or stick exercises in supine, sitting, or standing, for flexion-extension and horizontal abduction-adduction.
9. ROM-stretching exercise with hands-on assistance of aide.

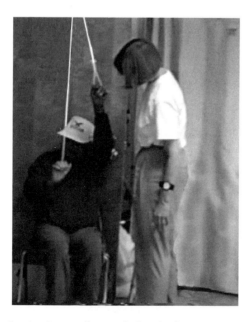

Figure 5–1   The patient is using a pulley attached to the door.

Figure 5–2 Using a finger ladder.

USE OF MOIST HEAT, ICE, AND MEDICATIONS

Moist heat to a stiff shoulder for 20 minutes before exercises increases the extensibility of shortened tissues[2] and may allow greater ROM. If the person is unusually sore, an analgesic such as acetaminophen or a nonsteroidal anti-inflammatory drug (NSAID) such as aspirin or ibuprofen may help. Although these medications do not require a physician's prescription, it is wise to consult with the physician because the patient may be taking medications that could have an adverse interaction with the nonprescription drug.

Moist heat for 20 minutes after exercise often relieves postexercise pain. To prevent burns instruct the aide in the cautious use of heat for patients with cognitive or communication problems or neurologic involvement. Some patients may prefer cold packs, but close monitoring is required because cold may be poorly tolerated by patients with circulatory problems. Other modalities can be used but must be administered by the physical therapist or a physical therapist assistant.

Figure 5–3 Clipping clothespins to a curtain.

ACTIVITIES OF DAILY LIVING

Evaluate the patient periodically, especially for ADL. Dressing, washing (especially axillae), combing and shampooing hair, reaching, and even eating can be impaired by a shoulder dysfunction.[3] Communicate with staff and the patient's family about what the patient is able to do for himself and how others may facilitate greater independence in ADL.

CASE REPORTS

The patients whose case reports follow benefit from a shoulder program three times a week.

Espisonio (Tony) F

Tony is a native of Puerto Rico and does not speak or understand English. He was admitted to the long-term care facility 15 years ago with organic brain syndrome, chronic convulsive disorder, and alcohol abuse. He was unable to care for himself in the community. Tony has two brothers and a sister

Figure 5–4   Batting a suspended ball with a bat.

who remain in contact with him. He is pleasant, though nonverbal. He usually walks with his head down, but when greeted in Spanish, Tony lifts his head and smiles. He is right-handed and is 82 years of age.

Tony sustained a fracture of the left humerus in a fall 8 months ago and was referred to physical therapy for ROM and strengthening exercises. Initially, passive ROM of the left shoulder was 60 degrees flexion, 45 degrees abduction, and 20 degrees external rotation. Right shoulder ROM was 160 degrees flexion, 160 degrees abduction, and 90 degrees external rotation. Elbow ROM was full. Muscle strength in flexion and abduction was 3/5 within available ROM. Tony had no functional use of the arm.

Tony participated in physical therapy for 1 month. Therapy consisted of moist heat, joint mobilization, and exercises. Passive ROM increased to 110 degrees flexion, 90 degrees external rotation, and 45 degrees external rotation. There was no change in strength, but Tony began to actively use the left arm as an assistive extremity. Tony reached a plateau in his progress and was discharged from direct physical therapy.

After a month without therapy, ROM was re-evaluated and found to have decreased. Tony, in the company of another patient with a shoulder disability, began a regular program of supervised exercises for the left upper extremity. These exercises are supervised by a physical therapy aide. ROM and function have improved to the level at which they were when the skilled program was stopped, and they have been maintained.

Rose T

Rose is 73 years of age. She was married and lived in the community, then suffered a cerebrovascular accident 3 years ago. She returned to her home in 6 weeks, but her mental status had deteriorated. Rose's her husband died 3 months later. Rose was admitted to the long-term care facility with a diagnosis of dementia and organic brain syndrome. Rose has two sons who visit often.

Medical diagnoses include diabetes mellitus and mitral valve disease. Rose is deaf but able to lip read. One year ago, she underwent a left modified radical mastectomy for cancer. She was referred to physical therapy for ROM and strengthening exercises for the left upper extremity.

ROM in the shoulder was flexion to 105 degrees, abduction to 90 degrees, internal rotation to 50 degrees, and external rotation to 25 degrees. Left elbow flexion was 15 to 150 degrees. Formal strength testing could not be conducted because of dementia, but functional strength in the shoulder was 3/5 in flexion and abduction within available ROM. Rose also had slight edema of the left hand and wrist.

Rose was generally nonverbal, but would indicate pain during stretching. She followed directions well, if they were cued physically and demonstrated to allow for her deafness. Rose received physical therapy for 1 month. Therapy consisted of moist heat followed by stretching, joint mobilization, and exercise to restore ROM and strength. Rose had improvements in ROM of 20 to 30 degrees in all planes. Elbow extension returned to full, and edema decreased. However, Rose still did not actively use her (nondominant) left hand for ADL. She was incapable of carrying out an independent exercise program.

Rose was placed on a maintenance program. She now comes to the physical therapy department with another patient with a shoulder disability, and under supervision of an aide, follows a series of exercises. These include the shoulder wheel, finger ladder, cane exercises, Codman pendulum, pulleys, batting a ball suspended on a string, and active exercise. She requires supervision, physical cues, and demonstration to carry out the exercises. ROM, strength, and functional use of the left arm have remained unchanged.

REFERENCES

1. Stableforth PG. Shoulder injuries in the elderly. In: Newman, RJ, ed. *Orthogeriatrics: Comprehensive orthopaedic care for the elderly patient.* Boston: Butterworth-Heinemann, 1992, pp.159-166.
2. Kisner C, Colby LA. *Therapeutic exercise: Foundations and techniques,* 2d ed. Philadelphia: Davis, 1990.
3. Goldstein TS. *Geriatric orthopedics: Rehabilitative management of common problems.* Gaithersburg: Aspen, 1991.

6

Severe Cognitive Impairment: Range of Motion and Positioning

A cognitive or psychiatric impairment, when severe, may result in disability involving ambulation, transfers, or activities of daily living (ADL).[1] Some patients are unable to participate in group exercises because of their degree of impairment. They may be unable to follow even one-step commands or may be disruptive to the group. These patients need a highly individualized program. Exercise is beneficial to these patients in maintaining strength and the ability to walk. It can also induce fatigue, which may help the person sleep better.

AMBULATION

Even in the presence of advanced senile dementia, the ability to walk is often retained. In walking, muscles and joints function together in coordinative structures that operate relatively automatically.[2] A person may forget how to speak, to dress and bathe herself, or even feed herself but may still be able to walk.

Whenever possible, the person should be assisted in walking every day. Apraxia, the inability to plan and execute a skilled movement,[3] can cause unsteadiness and difficulty walking. The person may be unable to learn the use of an assistive device, but can be led by the hand or walk with contact guard. A combination walker-frame and seat (Figure 6–1) may allow supervised, safe ambulation (Figure 6–2).

A person who is unable to use a walker or another assistive device may be able to walk in parallel bars. If the person is unable to walk at all, she should be assisted to stand every day, either in parallel bars or holding on to the hall railings. Daily standing promotes strength, postural control, and range of motion (ROM), especially in the ankles; prevents pressure ulcers; promotes pulmonary function and circulation; and maintains urinary and digestive systems. To document progress, record distance walked or time stood.

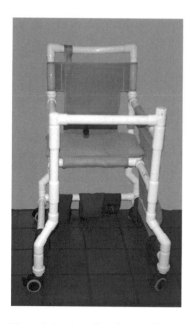

Figure 6–1 A walker frame with attached seat.

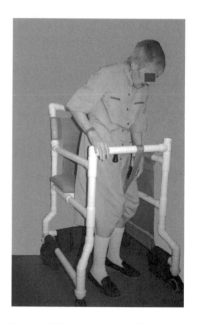

Figure 6–2 A patient walking with the walker frame. The base of the walker is weighted to stabilize it.

EXERCISE AND SENSORY STIMULATION

People who cannot follow commands can be given motor problems to solve. Unless doing so causes agitation, place a towel or pillowcase over the person's head, a blindfold over the eyes, or a rubber band around the fingers (Figure 6–3). The person's attempt to remove the object requires upper-extremity ROM, strength, coordination, and motor planning. Record how long it takes the person to perform the task. When possible, encourage function by handing the person a comb, a pencil, or an article of clothing to put on.

To stimulate tactile and vibratory senses, place a windup toy or other vibrating object in the person's hands. A vibrating ball or a pillow also can be used. Hand the person objects with varying textures or perhaps an ice cube. Hand cream also stimulates the tactile sense and facilitates bilateral use of the hands. There are commercially available kits with various textures and surfaces, but it is easy to make your own from objects around the house. Various fabrics, sandpaper, putty, and other objects and substances can be used.

A radio, music box, or doll with a string to make it talk provides auditory stimulation. Encourage the person to blow a whistle or ring a bell. Jingle balls and beeper balls are available. A flashlight in a dark room stimulates visual awareness. A mirror can encourage a person to attend to visual stimulation.

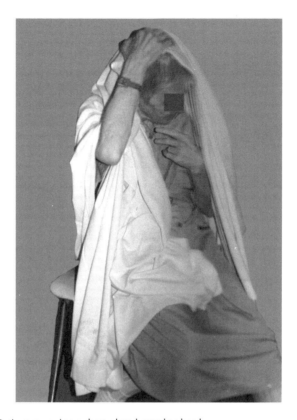

Figure 6–3   Patient removing a sheet placed over her head.

The olfactory sense is very primitive and can evoke memories and feelings in the distant or recent past.[1] The smell of cologne or disinfectant sprayed on a tissue, or cooking spices tied in a napkin can be effective. Moth balls, liniment, onion, peppermint, and other familiar odors can be used. Again, sensory evaluation kits are commercially available, but it is easy to make your own. It is best to use only two different smells at each session to avoid overstimulation.

CASE REPORT

The following patient is unable to participate in a group program because of the severity of her cognitive impairment, but she can walk with an appropriate device and perform some individualized activities.

Jane B

As a child, Jane was considered a tomboy and was very athletic. She was intelligent as well; she was the valedictorian of her high school class. Jane graduated from Pennsylvania State University having majored in chemistry and English literature. She married and worked for a few years as a chemist. She had two daughters and a son. According to Jane's older daughter, Jane's husband left the family 20 years ago, and the couple were divorced 7 years later. Jane became increasingly withdrawn, especially after the divorce. She lived with her daughter but began to have more difficulty caring for herself and had paranoid thoughts. Jane's daughter became unable to provide the care necessary, and Jane was admitted to a long-term care facility 10 years ago.

Jane is now 72 years of age. Her older daughter and son have remained interested in her care and visit often. Jane's diagnoses include Alzheimer's disease, seizure disorder, and tardive dyskinesia. Phenytoin is prescribed to control seizures. Jane has a history of falls in the past few years. She sustained a left hip fracture 3 years ago and a fracture of the left distal radius 18 months ago. She can walk short distances but is unsteady. Unattended, Jane tries to get up and has been knocked over by other patients. For this reason, she is seated in a wheelchair with a seat belt, which she cannot release. Jane is nonverbal, is incontinent, and is dependent for dressing, bathing, eating, and other self care. She was referred to physical therapy for evaluation.

The therapist found Jane's ROM was full; strength and balance testing was not possible because of the cognitive deficits. Jane was unable to follow commands, such as "stand up" or "come here." However, she was easily led by the hand with physical cues. Jane walked with short, shuffling steps with her head down. Unattended, Jane would walk aimlessly in circles. When led to a chair, she would appear confused and needed assistance to turn and sit down. When handed an object, Jane would not take it. She was unable to manipulate objects.

Jane did not have an acute onset of disability but was at risk for falls. The therapist deemed a maintenance program necessary to preserve Jane's ability to walk and transfer, maintain strength and endurance, and prevent falls. Because of her cognitive deficits, Jane could not participate in a group program. Instead, the therapist helps Jane transfer to a walker frame with an attached seat.[2] A strap runs from the seat to a bar across the front of the frame to help prevent falls. Under supervision, Jane can walk freely about the room using this assistive device for 1 to $1\frac{1}{2}$ hours a day. Typically, Jane stands, walks 5 to 10 feet, sits down for about 5 minutes, then gets up again. Although Jane is unable to participate in group exercises in the room, she is more alert when other people are around. The therapist also walks with Jane for about 30 feet, leading her by the hand. Jane can perform some motor problem solving, including removing a bracelet from her wrist.

Last spring, Jane became more lethargic and spent most of her time sitting on the walker frame seat. In the room there was a large fan mounted near the ceiling. The therapist discovered, by accident, that Jane was more alert with the fan on. The cool air on hot spring days seemed to wake her up.

Three months later, however, Jane again became extremely lethargic. The therapist reported this condition to the physician. Jane underwent tests and was found to have phenytoin toxicity. Typical adverse effects of phenytoin are confusion, sedation, dizziness, and cerebellar signs, including ataxia.[4] The dosage of phenytoin was reduced, and Jane became more alert.

Jane continues with the program. Her level of alertness varies, and there are times when she is unable to use the assistive device. However, she has not had any falls in the past year and is meeting the goals of therapy.

RANGE OF MOTION AND POSITIONING

If a person is at risk for joint contractures or already has contractures and has limited ability to move on his own, it is important to preserve ROM as much as possible. Contractures can cause pressure ulcers at the hips, sacrum, ischial tuberosities, heels, or elbows. Perineal care becomes difficult. And it can become almost impossible to position a person comfortably to allow him to perform any self care, even eating.

Passive ROM if done carefully can prevent further contractures. However, the therapist should assume that there is considerable likelihood of osteoporosis in a patient who must stay in bed. Patients with neurologic damage, especially a spinal cord injury, cannot provide feedback about pain. If there is also spasticity, ROM must be done cautiously and slowly to prevent fractures.

A decreased metabolic rate in the elderly may result in a lowered tissue temperature. Stretching is most effective when the muscles and connective tissues are warmed.[5] Contract-relax techniques can be used to increase circulation and prepare for stretching. Heating pads can be applied before stretching. However, patients with decreased cognition and communication abilities and patients with neurologic impairments are at risk for burns, so these patients must be very carefully monitored.

Positioning devices, such as a foot-drop splint, which positions the ankle in neutral, or knee-extension or hip-abduction splints can help maintain ROM.[5] Complex positioning or contracture problems are indications for consultation with an orthotist.

Patients with severe joint contractures require careful evaluation of sitting posture. A customized wheelchair can accommodate even the most severe joint contractures. In an adapted wheelchair, a person can be seated in the most erect position possible with head and trunk aligned. A person who is at risk for pressure ulcers requires a pressure-reducing seat cushion. If a pressure ulcer is already present, a pressure-relieving cushion is recommended. A geriatric chair or recliner is not compatible with these specialized seating requirements and cannot accommodate postural deformities. In addition, a person in a totally reclined position cannot interact with or even see most of the environment.

Patients with intact cognition but with severe contractures or weakness that prevent using a manual chair may be provided with a power wheelchair. Power wheelchairs with proper adaptations can afford independent mobility to a person who has very limited voluntary movement, perhaps only a finger or head.

CASE REPORTS

ROM and positioning can performed by an aide who has been carefully instructed, as illustrated by the following two case reports.

Fred D

Fred is the third child in an Italian family of 13 children. He never married and was employed as a laborer and caddy. He has a brother who lives in a distant state. Fred has been a resident in long-term care since 1983 and is 86 years of age.

Fred's medical history includes diabetes mellitus, left hemiplegia secondary to a cerebral vascular accident, left nephrectomy, hypertension, cancer of the prostate, and spinal fusion. Before the left nephrectomy, Fred could walk with some difficulty using a walker. However, after the operation, Fred could walk only minimally with staff assistance. Six months ago, Fred fell, sustaining fractures of the left hip and left humerus. Fred received an Austin Moore prosthetic hip replacement and shoulder immobilizer. Fred had many problems in the hospital, including pneumonia, a urinary tract infection, and pressure ulcers, which prolonged his recovery. Fred returned to the long-term care facility and was referred to physical therapy 2 months later.

At evaluation, Fred had multiple flexion contractures throughout with a severe increase in tone. Hip adductor spasticity made perineal care difficult. Fred did have limited active, but nonfunctional, movement of his right upper extremity and head. He had no active movement of his other extremities. The left hand was fisted, with the wrist ankylosed at 60 degrees of flexion. Fred had right wrist extension to neutral; left passive elbow flexion 35 to 90 degrees; right active elbow flexion 30 to 110 degrees; and bilateral shoulder flexion of 95 degrees. Lower extremity passive ROM was as follows: left knee flexion was 90 to 100 degrees; right knee flexion 30 to 90 degrees; left dorsiflexion to neutral; right plantar flexion contracture of 30 degrees. The left hip was postured in 10 degrees of adduction and 45 degrees of internal rotation. The right hip was in neutral abduction-adduction and 60 degrees of external rotation. Fred was completely dependent for transfers. He was awake and alert but did not say much—only "it hurts" at the end range of passive ROM.

Fred had a left ischial pressure ulcer 3.5 cm in diameter and 2.5 cm deep. The ulcer was surgically debrided several times as outpatient treatment at the acute care hospital. Eventually Fred underwent surgical closure of the wound.

Fred was unable to participate in an exercise program because of his almost complete lack of voluntary movement. He was unable to manipulate objects and was dependent for all self care. However, passive ROM and positioning were indicated to prevent further contractures and promote healing of the ulcer. Bilateral wrist splints were used to position the right wrist in 60 degrees of flexion and the left wrist in neutral. Fred wore these splints at night.

The therapist scheduled Fred for daily gentle ROM exercises to all four extremities and repositioning. This was assigned to a physical therapy aide with on-site supervision and monthly reassessments. Treatments were discussed with the aide carefully, because Fred can be presumed to have osteoporosis and is at risk for fractures. ROM is done only within Fred's pain-free tolerance. The aide has 25 years of experience and is competent to perform the treatments.

Fred was hospitalized 2 months ago with diagnoses of aspiration pneumonia, hyponatremia, and recurrent urinary tract infection. He resumed treatment on his return.

Fred is free of pressure ulcers. ROM has remained essentially unchanged.

Emily L

Emily had been living with her daughter and family until 7 years ago, when she became unable to care for herself. Emily is now 77 years of age. She has organic brain syndrome, alcoholic dementia, peripheral arteriosclerosis of the lower extremities, and cataracts.

At evaluation, the therapist found multiple joint contractures. Emily was resistant to ROM and was unable to participate in active exercises. She held her upper extremities in a flexed position, with passive elbow flexion of 10 to 90 degrees bilaterally and shoulder flexion of 90 degrees bilaterally. The left lower extremity was postured in an extension synergy with knee extension, hip adduction, and internal rotation. The left lower extremity was crossed over the right. Emily had right knee ROM of 20 to 90 degrees. The left hip was adducted 10 degrees; left hip flexion was to 60 degrees; and left knee flexion was to 30 degrees. Emily was unable to sit in a wheelchair because of joint contractures and was reclined in a geriatric chair.

Her slight build and the multiple joint contractures placed Emily at risk for skin ulceration. In addition, spasticity of the abductor muscles of the left hip made perineal hygiene difficult. A hip abductor splint was recommended and obtained to help stretch the hip adductor muscles safely. Nurses apply the splint.

Emily participates in physical therapy for ROM exercises and repositioning in the geriatric chair or bed to prevent further contractures and skin ulcerations. This is done by a physical therapy aide with on-site supervision and periodic re-evaluation by the therapist. Because of the likelihood of osteoporosis, the exercises are done only slowly and carefully, within pain-free limits. ROM and skin integrity have been preserved.

SUMMARY

People with severe cognitive or psychiatric impairments may or may not have a mobility dysfunction. If a person is able to move safely in his environment, physical therapy intervention may not be needed. If a person can walk but is unsafe, the therapist can identify environmental risks and suggest interventions by the caregiver to improve safety.

For a person who is able to walk but needs help, a maintenance program, perhaps using an assistive device, is indicated. Because the ability to learn and apply new information is impaired, a person may be unable to use a walker or cane. Ambulation with contact guard or using a walker frame may be necessary.

Patients who cannot walk and spend the day either sitting or in bed are at risk for joint contractures and the loss of remaining functional abilities. A program of ROM, sensory stimulation, and exercise within a person's ability to participate are beneficial.

Timely physical therapy intervention can prevent the end-stage complications of immobility, including joint contractures and pressure ulcers. If joint contractures do occur, the therapist can work with nurses on positioning or orthotic devices. If pressure ulcers occur, the therapist may consider using modalities, such as whirlpool, electrical stimulation, or ultrasound.[6–10]

The program requires the assessment skills of the physical therapist to be established, but it can be carried out by others with periodic supervision. Declines in cognitive and functional abilities may be rapid or gradual, and medical complications are often frequent. The therapist must periodically reevaluate and change the program as needed.

SUPPLIERS

Walker Frame with Attached Seat

Merry Walker
Merry Walker Corporation
1357 Northmoor Ct
Northbrook, IL 60062
708-498-9028

Ambi-Walker
Custom Durable Products, Inc.
53040 Faith Ave
Elkhart, IN 46514
800-933-0256

Alco Ambulator
6851 High Grove Blvd
Burr Ridge IL 60521
800-323-4282

Vibrating Balls, Jingle balls, Beeper balls

Sportime Abilitation
One Sportime Way
Atlanta, GA 30340
800-283-5700

Tactile Stimulation Kit

Sammons Inc.
P.O. Box 386
Western Springs, IL 60558-0386
800-323-5547

Flaghouse Rehab
150 N. MacQuesten Pkwy
Mt. Vernon NY 10550
800-793-7900

Sensory Evaluation Kit

Sportime Abilitation
One Sportime Way
Atlanta, GA 30340
800-283-5700

Foot-ankle Positioning Splints, Hip Abductor Splints

Susquehanna Rehab Products
RD 2 Box 41
Wrightsville, PA 17368
800-248-2011

Sammons Inc.
P.O. Box 386
Western Springs, IL 60558-0386
800-323-5547

Smith and Nephew Rolyan
P.O. Box 555
Menomonee Falls, WI 53052-0555
800-558-8633

REFERENCES

1. Mace NL, Hardy SR, Rabins PV. Alzheimer's disease and the confused patient. In: Jackson O, ed. *Physical therapy of the geriatric patient,* 2d ed. *Clinics in Physical Therapy,* Vol. 21. New York: Churchill Livingstone, 1989, pp. 129-144.
2. Ward C. Learning and skill acquisition. In: Greenwood R, ed. *Neurological rehabilitation.* New York: Churchill Livingstone, 1993, pp. 111-124.
3. Goodgold-Edwards SA, Cermak SA. Integrating motor control and motor learning concepts with neuropsychological perspectives on apraxia and developmental apraxia. *Am J Occup Ther* 1989;44:431-439.
4. Ciccone, CD. *Pharmacology in rehabilitation.* Philadelphia: Davis, 1990.
5. Kisner C, Colby LA. *Therapeutic exercise: Foundations and techniques,* 2d ed. Philadelphia: Davis, 1990.
6. Fitzgerald GK, Newsome D. Treatment of a large infected thoracic spine wound using high voltage pulsed monophasic current. *Phys Ther* 1993;73:355-360.
7. Szuminsky NJ, Albers AC, Unger P, Eddy JG. Effect of narrow, pulsed high voltage on bacterial viability. *Phys Ther* 1994;74:660-667.
8. Nussbaum EL, Biemann I, Mustard B. Comparison of ultrasound/ultraviolet-C and laser for treatment of pressure ulcers in patients with spinal cord injury. *Phys Ther* 1994;74:812-825.
9. Hecox B, Mehreteab TA, Weisberg J. *Physical agents: A comprehensive manual for physical therapists.* East Norwalk: Appleton & Lange, 1994.
10. Kloth LC, McCulloch JM, Feeder JA. *Wound healing: Alternatives in management,* 2d ed. Philadelphia: Davis, 1994.

7

Communication and Motivation

Working with patients in small groups offers the advantage of efficiency. Treatment can be provided to more patients in the same amount of time than if the facilitator worked with each patient individually.

Group work provides benefits for the patients. The common preconception that the elderly cannot participate in groups is not true. Even confused patients are able to participate in programs designed for them.[1] Social interaction and stimulation, friendship, and communication with peers are just a few of the benefits of a group exercise program.

The supervising physical therapist should instruct the group facilitator or aide in the general dynamics of working with a group and in the exercise prescription as it applies to the needs of individual patients.

GENERAL PRINCIPLES IN GROUP WORK

Preparation of the Room and Materials

Set up the room and materials in advance. Also, be sure to plan each day's activities. The program must be set up to meet the needs of the participants. Repetition of activities is useful in reinforcing what is learned but is boring if overdone.

Preparation of Participants

All patients need to wear appropriate shoes, clothing, glasses, and hearing aids when needed. While greeting everyone, orient participants by discussing the time, date, or weather. Psychological preparation about the purpose of the exercises is important. Nurses can often help by reminding a confused patient of the session an hour or so in advance.

What Name to Use?

This is usually the first question that arises when you meet a patient—or anyone else for that matter. When introducing yourself, encourage the patient to use your first name. This is appropriate if you are younger than the patient. Begin by using *Mr.*, *Mrs.*, or *Miss* in addressing the patient, but later ask what he or she prefers to be called, especially if others are using first names. If a patient invites you to use his first name, do so; otherwise continue to use the honorific.

A nonverbal patient may be unable to tell you how he or she prefers to be addressed. You can convey your feeling of respect for these patients by using *Mr.*, *Mrs.*, or *Miss*. Some patients may feel the use of a first name is too familiar, especially during the initial meeting.

At many facilities, it is common for the nurses and others to call the patients by their first names. If the person's family is available, ask their advice. If not, use the form of address that others do. Consistency in address among staff members may help a confused patient cope with new and unfamiliar surroundings.

Coordination with Nursing, Other Services

Check with the nurses or read the patient's chart before each session. This does not need to be a time-consuming process, but it is important to know if there has been any change or event that would affect therapy.

Communication

As you assemble the group, greet everyone by name. Begin with some informal conversation with participants concerning the weather, season, news, future events, or holidays just past or coming up. Be sure to make eye contact; you need to sit down in front of the person. Avoid looking down on someone while speaking to him. Lightly touching the person's hand or shoulder while speaking to him may aid communication. Encourage socialization and learning of others' names by members of the group. In conversation, be sure you do not reveal confidential information about any patient to others in the group.

When introducing an activity, make explanations simple and brief. Demonstrate each exercise first. Ask the patient whom you expect to have the least difficulty to go first with a new activity. Make it clear that you do not expect a perfect performance and be liberal with praise for effort.

Whenever possible, do not undermine a patient's confidence by correcting her, especially in front of others. Instead, demonstrate correct technique again. Accept some blame for a mistake when you can; for example, say, "I didn't explain that very well." Corrections must be handled tactfully and should be made only when absolutely necessary.

If a patient is performing a transfer in an unsafe manner, it is necessary to correct him to avoid reinforcing the mistake. However, make the correction in positive terms whenever possible. For example, "You did get up yourself, but a safer way to do it is . . . ." Even better is to help the person avoid a mistake by providing oral instruction and cues throughout the activity.

If a patient is having difficulty, you can probably break the task down into simpler elements. Be sure to tell the patient you know how difficult the task is while expressing confidence in the patient's ability to one day master it. Effort and willingness to try are the important factors.

At the end of the session, express appreciation to all for their attendance and remind them of the next session.

Motivation

Aerobics and physical fitness are much in style. However, our elderly patients grew up in a society that did not value exercise for its own sake.[2] They may have been very active physically when young but in purposeful activities, such as earning a living or keeping house without modern conveniences. They may not easily accept exercise for fitness.

Today many people enjoy activities and games for fun. But many older people see games as something for children. Be careful to present activities in non-demeaning, non-childish ways. It helps to explain the purpose of the exercise—to improve strength in the legs and improve walking, for example.

Using a stuffed animal or toy is suggested for some activities, but may be inappropriate for some patients. A stuffed toy per se is not childish; these toys are often marketed to and collected by adults. Some women, in particular, are charmed by dolls. Dolls can be used to reinforce identification of body parts and communication and are evocative of memories, both personal and family. Still, if a patient should object to or be uncomfortable with any activity they perceive as childish, his or her feelings must be recognized and accepted.

Some patients may be embarrassed or self-conscious in front of a group. They may fear not doing as well as others or incurring the disapproval of the group leader. Try to foster an atmosphere of acceptance and safety.

Some activities, such as decorating a Christmas tree or an Easter egg hunt, may have therapeutic benefits, but they could offend religious sensibilities. Be aware of and respectful of cultural and religious differences.

SPECIAL PROBLEMS

Obstacles may arise during a session. Prepare for and anticipate the following situations.

Interruptions

Sometimes a participant forgets his glasses or needs to visit the bathroom during a session. It takes two facilitators to handle a group safely, especially if some participants are confused or unable to walk safely alone.

Nurses may interrupt the group to administer medications or take vital signs. Request that whenever possible these procedures be attended to either before or after the group activity.

A patient may report pain or shortness of breath during an activity. Neither is normal. Stop the activity. If the pain continues or the shortness of breath does not resolve quickly, notify the nurse and physician.

Joint pain, especially in the back, hips, or knees often accompanies arthritic changes. Unfortunately, chronic joint pain can limit mobility and is often not treated easily. Consult with the physician about treatment. A patient's reports of pain must be understood and respected. She may need reassurance that it is safe to exercise even in the presence of occasional joint pain. An exacerbation of chronic pain may require a short-term course of modalities, splinting, rest, or specific range of motion (ROM) exercises to preserve mobility.

The Confused Patient: Reality Orientation versus Validation Therapy

Despite efforts to orient a patient to what is occurring during a session, he may be confused, and this may limit his participation. He may not comprehend instructions. Verbalizations may be incoherent, illogical, confused, or the patient may not speak at all.

Avoid patronizing a confused person. Although he may not be verbal, he may sense a condescending attitude and not want to be spoken to as a child. Do not oversimplify vocabulary, use a singsong voice, or otherwise talk down to the person. If he has difficulty understanding language, substitute nonverbal communication, such as physical cues, gestures, and touch.

Reality orientation is a program of repetitive, orienting activities carried out by all staff members who have contact with the patient. It works well for patients who are temporarily confused, as may occur on initial adjustment to a change in living arrangements. Gently reminding a person of present reality may help him adapt to a new environment.

However, the person in the latter stages of Alzheimer's disease never recovers from chronic dementia. It is futile to try to force the patient to confront the truth and may cause him to withdraw further or become hostile.

Validation therapy, developed by Naomi Feil, MSW,[3] is an alternative to reality therapy. It is based on responding to the feelings a patient is trying to communicate and not the actual words. For example, by asking for a deceased spouse, a person may be expressing loneliness or sadness. Instead of insistently reminding the patient his spouse is dead, assure him that he is cared for and valued where he is.

With this approach, it is important to listen with full attention as you talk with the patient. Express the emotional need aloud, affirming the person's right to both have and express feelings. With a person who is using jargon, invented words, or gestures, it may help to repeat the words or gestures to the patient to draw out his feelings. Attempt to create a feeling of empathy.

One study suggested that confused patients often respond to this approach better in a group setting than outside a group. They are able to share feelings and problems, follow a theme, and interact well with others.[4] Sensitive listening and partial entry into the patient's reality may be effective in preventing anxiety-related outbursts and behavior problems.[5]

Patients' feelings often relate to a need to belong, to be useful, or to express strong emotions. Discuss delusions as memories rather than reality. It is far more humane to reassure a patient he is safe and respected than to vigorously insist that he accept a reality he can no longer comprehend.

The Disruptive Patient

A patient who disrupts an activity with loud or inappropriate conversation or gestures can interfere with and compromise the safety and success of the program. Try to determine if the behavior is unusual for the patient. If it is not, determine if others have found successful methods of dealing with the behavior.

There is always a reason for behavior. Rather than labeling a patient as manipulative or difficult, approach the behavior as a detective would and try to determine the reason for it. This allows for objectivity and avoids a power struggle with the patient. Possible reasons may be frustration, attention seeking, or a simple refusal to participate.

Just as open-ended questions and comments can be used to draw out a shy, withdrawn person, sometimes closed-end statements and firm instruction can be used to redirect, quiet, and calm a disruptive patient.

The Patient Who Refuses to Participate

Discuss privately with the patient who refuses to participate her personal goals, especially concerning mobility and strength. Everyone, regardless of age, desires autonomy and independence. Relate this to very specific, short-term objectives of the therapy program. An authoritarian approach is not useful; the patient needs to be a part of the decision making process and must feel she is in control. It is useful to concentrate on the physical rather than the psychologic benefits associated with exercise.

Avoid coercion, bribes, or manipulation. These may work temporarily but are ultimately not respectful of the person, and they fail in the long term.

Ultimately, a patient has the right to refuse to participate, and this decision must be respected. Be sure to leave the door open to a patient who later changes her mind.

The Patient with a Sensory Impairment

In the visual system, the most important age-related ocular disease is presbyopia, or difficulty focusing on close objects. This often requires the wearing of bi- or trifocal glasses. These glasses can cause difficulty with ambulation, especially on curbs and steps, where the person uses mid-range vision to focus on the edge of the step and far vision to focus on the horizon to orient his posture. Misperception can result in a fall. Other common ocular diseases among the elderly include cataracts, glaucoma, diabetic retinopathy, and macular degeneration.

The acuity of both the *distance senses* (vision and hearing) and the *body senses* (somatosensory, vestibular, and proprioception) decrease in the elderly.[6] A study has shown that elderly fallers tend to rely on vision more than do non-fallers.[7] Another study suggested input from the ankle is more important than visual information in preventing falls.[8] Encourage patients to rely on their less-impaired senses.

A patient with a visual deficit can be encouraged to better attend to auditory information by, for example, identifying environmental sounds on a tape recording. Avoid startling such a patient by speaking to her as you approach. Clapping hands, music, or other cues may help orient the person to what is happening in the room.

Listening aids can help a person with an auditory impairment, but it may be difficult for the person to put them on without assistance. Help the person. Speak clearly in a deep voice, because high frequencies are usually most affected in a hearing loss. Don't shout. Communicate with touch and with gestures.

The senses of touch, smell, and taste also decline with age.[9,10] Encourage touch and the use of the hands by asking the patient to identify objects placed in his hand. Ask patients to identify various odors, such as flowers, bleach, and coffee.

Getting Personal

Professionals who work with an elderly disabled person need to think through personal attitudes concerning aging and disability. Essential are a respect for the uniqueness and value of the person and avoiding a judgment on the quality of life of others.

To make a connection, it may be helpful to share aspects of one's private life. Talking about family or a shared hobby may promote a therapeutic relationship. Be sure not to burden the patient with personal problems, however.

Although psychologic benefits may accompany group exercises, without psychologic training it is better to avoid all forms of talk therapy. Concentrate instead on the goal-directed physical aspects of the program.

CASE REPORTS

The following four reports illustrate difficulties with communication and motivation. The first two examples show that not every case ends with success.

Lillian A

Lillian, now 55 years of age, was married at 18 years of age and is widowed. She was a factory worker. Lillian has a son and a daughter who visit occasionally. The medical diagnoses include chronic obstructive pulmonary disease, insulin-dependent diabetes mellitus, hypertension, atherosclerotic heart disease, and peripheral vascular disease. The peripheral vascular disease led to osteomyelitis and above-knee amputations on the right 5 years ago and the left 1 year later. Lillian has a history of pressure ulcers of the coccyx. She is occasionally incontinent of bowel and bladder. Despite her medical problems, Lillian has continued to smoke half a pack of cigarettes a day and does not wish to stop. In fact, she seeks more cigarettes from others whenever she can. She has been a resident of a long-term care facility for 3 years.

Lillian was referred to physical therapy on nursing request. At evaluation, the therapist found bed mobility was independent with a trapeze. Transfers to and from bed, wheelchair, and toilet were with supervision only. Wheelchair mobility was independent. Upper extremity muscle strength was 5/5 (Lillian could execute sitting push-ups independently). Skin condition was intact. Although Lillian had hip flexion contractures of 35 degrees, this is to be expected in a patient who must stay in a wheelchair and did not interfere with function. Lillian was quite independent with all activities of daily living and mobility at the wheelchair level.

The nurse reported that Lillian was frequently depressed and withdrew from contact with others. Sometimes this behavior escalated until Lillian refused to eat. The nurse had noticed emotional benefits in some patients who participated in exercises and hoped that the exercises would counteract Lillian's depression.

The therapist was reluctant to have Lillian join the group. For one thing, her cognition was intact, and many activities might prove too simple for her. And Lillian could not participate in lower-extremity exercises. More important, just as one would not expect a psychiatrist to treat a physical disability, physical therapy is not treatment of depression.

Nevertheless, the therapist agreed to let Lillian try group exercise and tried to make the activities interesting for her. Despite this, Lillian began to ask to leave early, and after 2 weeks was refusing to participate at all. The therapist discussed this with the nurse, who said she had been seeing an improvement in Lillian's mood since she began therapy. The nurse also remarked that Lillian seemed stronger and more willing to transfer to the toilet regularly. Then the nurse suggested that Lillian's cigarettes be withheld if Lillian refused to participate. Lillian had been routinely bribed in this way to get her to attend recreational therapy and to follow many routines of the day. This practice was discussed with Lillian's physician. He also believed the benefits of exercise justified the manipulation.

The therapist did not agree with the practice of withholding cigarettes but after consideration went along with the practice for 2 more weeks. At the end of the 2 weeks, the therapist discussed the situation with Lillian. The therapist told Lillian she valued her participation but did not want to bribe her anymore. The therapist asked Lillian if there were activities that would make exercise more interesting for her, or if she would like to participate in individual exercises instead of the group. She said no, she didn't like to exercise at all and would do so only if she had to in order to get cigarettes. The therapist told the nurse and the physician of Lillian's desire not to participate and she was discharged from the group exercise program.

Jean R

Jean is 75 years of age, admitted to the long-term care facility a year and a half ago with a diagnosis of Alzheimer's disease. She has a daughter who visits occasionally. Medical diagnoses include thrombocytopenia, tardive dyskinesia with akathisia, anemia, and controlled hypertension. She is confused and nonverbal.

Jean was independent in all ambulation and transfers without an assistive device until it was noticed 1 year ago that she was having difficulty walking. There was no known injury or fall, but radiographs revealed a comminuted fracture of the left hip. Jean underwent open reduction internal fixation of the hip. She was referred to physical therapy 1 week later for transfer and non–weight-bearing gait training and exercise.

Although she could not speak, Jean could follow verbal and physical cues. Left hip flexion was limited to 75 degrees; knee flexion to 40 degrees. Jean indicated pain with ROM of both hip and knee. Left quadriceps strength was 3–/5, hip flexors 2/5, and hip abduction 2/5. Jean could execute a straight leg raise on the right but not the left. Other strength and ROM values were within functional limits. Transfers from supine to sitting required moderate assistance to move the left lower extremity. Stand pivot transfers required moderate assist of one to maintain non–weight-bearing status.

Jean could understand and comply with non–weight-bearing instruction and progressed from the parallel bars to a walker. In 1 month, she was allowed partial weight-bearing. She continued to progress with ambulation, and in another month was walking with full weight-bearing using a straight cane. However, her balance was impaired, primarily by her akathisia (motor restlessness), best described in Jean as fidgety.

Jean had many extraneous movements of her extremities. She reached for another person abruptly while walking, shifting her cane from the right to left hand while doing so, and sometimes staggered to one side or the other. She required only supervision to walk, but it was best for the helper stand behind her, and not too close, or Jean tried to reach for an arm.

Jean could maintain her balance on either foot (single limb stance) with one-handed support using the cane for 5 seconds. She could ascend and descend steps foot over foot with only close supervision using a railing and the straight cane. Jean was resistant to ROM exercises for the hip and knee. Hip flexion improved to 90 degrees only, and knee flexion to 100 degrees.

The physician diagnosed heterotopic ossification of the left hip of unknown causation and recommended continued ROM exercises. Jean consistently expressed pain during stretching. Because of Jean's age, thin build, and fair skin, the risk of osteoporosis was high,[11] and aggressive ROM was contraindicated. Hip flexion continued to be a problem, especially during transfers from sitting to standing, because Jean had to lean far to the right side (away from the left hip) to bring her center of gravity over her feet.

After 2 months of physical therapy, Jean reached a plateau in her progress. She required close supervision for transfers because of the limitation in hip flexion and far supervision for ambulation with the straight cane. She remained at moderate risk for falls, because of her akathisia and distractibility. Jean sometimes got up without the cane and tried to walk by holding on to a wall or furniture or reached for another person. Jean scored 2/7 on the Mobility Performance Scale (MPS) (see Chapter 8). Functional reach (FR) (see Chapter 8) could not be tested because Jean was unable to follow instructions. Jean was also unaware of the risks of walking with her shoes untied or walking on wet floors.

Jean joined a group exercise class. Safe technique was reinforced during ambulation and transfers. She participated well for 4 months, but gradually became increasingly resistant. She often got up to leave during a session; she tried to sneak away while the facilitator was occupied with another patient. This behavior was dangerous for Jean, and she was discharged from the exercise program. Jean continues to be at risk for falls. The nurses have been instructed in the level of supervision Jean requires for safety. She has not had any falls since leaving the program.

William C

William is 79 years of age and has a hearing impairment. He was admitted to a long-term care unit 7 years ago. At that time, reports were that he was in a wheelchair most of the time, but could walk with a strange gait, pushing his wheelchair, and was short-winded. William's medical diagnoses include angina pectoris, atherosclerotic heart disease, and hypertension.

The physician referred William to therapy because of an increased difficulty with transfers. At evaluation, William was seated in a wheelchair without footrests, which he could propel independently using both hands and his left foot. William's right knee was extended with his right foot in equinovarus. The foot could be passively positioned in neutral, but no active movement could be elicited. He had decreased strength in his back and hip extensor muscles. Other ROM and strength were within functional limits.

William had severe edema of both ankles, the right more than the left. He was initially very resistant to standing; he complained of "sand" in his leg (possibly meaning arthritis) and he also complained about his shoes. Eventually William was persuaded to stand and walk 5 feet. However, weight-bearing was entirely on the lateral border of the foot, and the therapist was unable to bring the right foot to a plantigrade position in standing. William was referred to the orthopedic surgeon. Electromyography revealed a generalized peripheral neuropathy and right peroneal nerve palsy of unknown causation. William was fitted with a molded ankle foot orthosis and new sneakers.

The therapist began helping William with ambulation in the parallel bars. Although he was initially resistant, William progressed to a wheeled walker over the next few days. One problem during therapy was that William did not like to be touched while walking, but he did need contact guarding for safety at first. The therapist simply told William she had to follow the rules of the facility. He was proud, even defensive at times. It probably helped to avoid any mention of his gait problems.

William did progress and in 2 weeks could transfer from sitting to standing and walk 50 feet with a wheeled walker with close supervision only. At first William exhibited a decrease in step length on the left, because of an inadequate push-off on the right. This gait problem has gradually resolved as William has become accustomed to the orthosis. William also tends to walk with his trunk flexed over his hips about 30 degrees, which may be the result of weakness of the back and hip extensors.

The therapist could not test FR, because William could not maintain standing independently without support. Transfers from standing to sitting initially were troublesome, because William refused to turn around completely and back up but dived for the chair. He often became angry with instruction. This too has gradually improved. Although William stubbornly refused to follow directions when they were given, he performed the activity correctly the next day when he did not feel threatened. The therapist then praised him lavishly.

The therapist found a wheelchair with footrests for William and tried to persuade him to use the footrests and propel the chair by pushing with his hands on the wheel rims only. This would better position both ankles and knees and prevent contractures. However, William adamantly refused the footrests. He continued to propel the chair using his left foot and his hands on the wheels. At least the orthosis does maintain the right ankle in good position. William is again able to transfer independently.

In 1 month, William progressed to the point where he no longer required an individualized program but could participate in group exercises to reinforce his transfer and maintain ambulation skills. He scored 2/7 on the MPS. FR could not be tested because William was unable to maintain standing balance while shifting weight. The therapist approaches new activities slowly with William, because he can be resistant at first. He is cooperative about coming to the group sessions and is meeting the maintenance goals of therapy.

Marie M

Marie is 45 years of age and has been a resident of a long-term care unit for the last 10 years. Her physical disabilities include Friedreich ataxia, organic brain syndrome, optic atrophy (she is legally blind), and obesity.

Marie is nonambulatory and has no active movement of her lower extremities. She has severe fixed equinovarus deformities of both ankles. The left ankle is ankylosed at 35 degrees and the right at 40 degrees of plantar flexion. Marie does have full active ROM of her upper extremities, but movement is uncoordinated and apraxic.

Marie is dependent for all transfers, dressing, and most self-feeding, although she can manage finger foods. Marie sits in a conventional wheelchair with a tray and has two dolls she likes to keep with her. Marie sometimes nods or shakes her head in response to questions, but is nonverbal. Marie is usually cooperative, but she becomes upset if her dolls are misplaced or if she is awakened from a nap. In these situations, she sometimes screams unintelligibly. Marie was referred for physical therapy evaluation for muscle strengthening and ROM exercises.

Marie joined a group exercise class. Goals of therapy include maintaining her ROM, strength, and functional abilities. In therapy, Marie can reach for and pass an object, but with difficulty because of her visual deficits. Marie can manipulate an object placed on her tray and can hook two Lego blocks together. She can touch places on her body on request and enjoys resistive exercises for her arms using Theraband. Marie cannot catch a ball but can locate and retrieve one from her wheelchair tray or lap. She can throw a ball awkwardly. Clapping hands or calling to her helps Marie localize and throw more accurately. Marie also receives passive ROM (stretching) exercises for her lower extremities.

Marie's wheelchair was worn. The upholstery was loose, the wheelrims were coming off, and the standard-width wheelchair was too narrow. The wheelchair needed replacement. The therapist recommended an extra wide chair with solid seat and back to improve posture, removable armrests to assist staff with transfers, swingaway elevating leg rests to allow occasional positioning of her knees in extension to maintain ROM, a tray, and a seat belt. Marie cannot manage the leg rests. However, she can propel and maneuver the wheelchair with auditory cues and encouragement and can lock and unlock the brakes with verbal and physical cues. However, the nurses usually pushed Marie in her wheelchair to the dining room, her bedroom, and other rooms.

The therapist decided to feature Marie on videotape and showed her pushing and maneuvering her wheelchair with cues and encouragement only. The therapist showed the tape to Marie, and although she probably could not see it clearly, she responded well to the attention and encouragement. Later, as part of in-service training, the therapist showed the tape to the staff on both the day and evening shifts. Most of the staff were quite surprised to learn how capable Marie is with her chair and have begun to ask her to push herself to activities.

Marie now pushes her wheelchair to therapy herself (with encouragement) and actively participates and enjoys the activities.

REFERENCES

1. Abraham IL, Niles SA. Therapeutic group work with depressed elderly. *Nurs Clin North Am* 1991;26:635–650.
2. Nelson D, Stucky, C. The roles of occupational therapy in preventing further disability of elderly persons in long term care facilities. In: Rothman J, Levine R, eds. *Prevention Practice: Strategies in Physical Therapy and Occupational Therapy*. Philadelphia: Saunders, 1992, pp. 19–35.
3. Feil N. Validation therapy. *Geriatr Nurs* 1992;13:129–133.

4. Bleathman C, Morton I. Validation therapy: Extracts from 20 groups with dementia sufferers. *J Adv Nurs* 1992;17:658–666.
5. Bohling HR. Communication with Alzheimer's patients: An analysis of caregiver listening patterns. *Int J Aging Hum Dev* 1991;33:249–267.
6. Whipple R, Woldson L, Derby C, Singh D, Tobin J. Altered sensory function and balance in older persons. *J Gerontol* 1993;48:71–76.
7. Lord SR, Webster IW. Visual field dependence in elderly fallers and non fallers. *Int J Aging Hum Dev* 1990;31:267–277.
8. Anacker SL, DiFabio RP. Influence of sensory inputs on standing balance in community-dwelling elders with a recent history of falling. *Phys Ther* 1992;72:575–581.
9. Lewis CB, Bottomley JM. *Geriatric physical therapy: A clinical approach.* Norwalk: Appleton & Lange, 1994.
10. Maguire GH. The changing realm of the senses. In: Lewis CB, ed. *Aging: The health care challenge,* 2d ed. Philadelphia: Davis, 1990.
11. Melton LJ III. Epidemiology of age-related fractures. In: Avioli LV, ed. *The osteoporotic syndrome: Detection,* prevention, and treatment, 3rd ed. New York: Wiley-Liss, 1993.

8

Preventing Falls and
Maximizing Independence

FALLS AMONG THE ELDERLY: INCIDENCE, ETIOLOGY, AND RISK FACTORS

Studies show that falls are the leading cause of fatal and nonfatal injuries among the elderly in the United States.[1,2] As many as 28 to 45 percent of community-dwelling elders and 45 to 61 percent of elders residing in nursing homes fall every year.[2] Some falls are fatal, and others result in serious injuries, including fractures of the femur, wrist, humerus, pelvis, and vertebral bodies. In fact, falls and injuries are the second leading cause of accidental death among people older than over 75 years of age.[3]

The incidence of falls is more common among elderly living in nursing homes than among the general population. In addition, falls more often result in serious injury of nursing home residents.[2,4]

Many factors are correlated with an increased risk of falls. Decreased balance, leg strength, and flexibility;[5] a low amount of daily motion;[6] poor self-perceived health;[6] and well-advanced age[6,7] correlate with a high rate of falls. Previous falls[7] and polypharmacy,[7,8] especially psychotropic medications,[9] are associated with increased risk. Other factors include depression, motivation, social isolation, and maladaptive behavior.[10] Cognitive impairment is positively correlated with a high risk for falls.[7,11-13] Among people with cognitive impairments and depression, it may be a discrepancy between actual and perceived balance that leads the person to perform activities that are unsafe and cause falls.[12]

A fall is usually the result of a combination of factors that relate to both the person and the environment.[1,14,15] A change in the environment is often effective intervention. Improvement of even a few of the risk factors, or simple modifications to the environment may be effective in reducing falls.[1,14-16]

The first step in examining a person with a history of falls is to identify treatable conditions, such as poor vision, muscle weakness, or a balance deficit. Then identify and modify other factors, including environmental factors, that may be contributory.[14,15]

CASE REPORTS

Falls were a problem for the patients in the following case reports.

Richard W

Richard is 72 years of age and has been a resident of a long-term care unit for 8 years. He has had a seizure disorder since the age of 16. His medical history includes a craniotomy for control of seizures, a cardiac operation for mitral stenosis. He sustained a left parietal skull fracture 5 years ago. After the skull fracture, Richard presented signs of ataxia. Since then, he has been essentially nonambulatory, although he has been independent at the wheelchair level, including transfers to and from bed and toilet. Richard carries a helmet with him at all times, but he had been told he needs it only when he is outside.

Richard was referred to physical therapy 4 months ago. He had fallen several times, most recently 2 weeks ago. In that fall he sustained a laceration on the right frontal area of his head. He had not been wearing the helmet. According to the nurses, Richard fell while trying to get into bed by putting his feet onto the bed first, rather than using the stand-pivot transfer he had used previously.

At evaluation, Richard denied any vertigo and seemed to minimize any difficulty with balance. Muscle strength in the quadriceps and gluteals was 4/5. Other muscle strength was 5/5 and range of motion (ROM) was full. Static standing balance was fair; Richard could maintain independent standing only with two-handed support. Dynamic balance was poor; Richard required contact guarding to perform a minimal weight shift. Functional reach (FR) could not be tested. Richard could walk in the parallel bars with contact guarding, but his gait was extremely ataxic, with a wide base of support and exaggerated hip flexion.

Richard participated in individual physical therapy sessions for 3 weeks. Treatment consisted of gait training with a wheeled walker, instruction in stand-pivot transfers, and gait, balance, and coordination training. The therapist also recommended Richard use the helmet during transfers. By the end of 3 weeks, Richard was again transferring independently. He was ambulatory with a wheeled walker for more than 200 feet with close supervision. However, Richard often moved impulsively—for example, to pick up something from the floor he had dropped—or he become agitated by other patients. Therefore, the therapist concluded he would never become completely independent with the walker but would require supervision to use it.

Richard joined a group exercise program to maintain his ability to transfer and walk. He was often anxious about his "heart condition" during therapy, but he did not report any chest discomfort during activities. At first resistant to participation, Richard began to relax and interact with other patients in a positive way.

A month ago, Richard was hospitalized for 5 days with severe anemia. He was treated medically for gastric ulcers and again referred for therapy. Richard was quite debilitated after more than a week of bed rest. He was short of breath after walking only 20 feet. Richard's balance had also declined, especially when he turned with the walker. He again received 5 days of individual physical therapy that emphasized endurance, transfers, and gait training with the goal of returning to the level of function before hospitalization. Richard was soon able to reach his goal.

Richard returned to the group. Again, he was at first resistant and anxious, but has begun to talk to others more and participates willingly. To reassure Richard about his heart, the therapist takes his pulse occasionally, although his mitral valve operation was more than 40 years ago and he does not have any ongoing cardiac problems. Richard's balance has improved; he is now able to maintain single limb stance (SLS) with one-handed support for 8 to 10 seconds, though he is unsteady. FR is 3 inches, which indicates an eight times greater than average risk of falls. However, Richard has not fallen since he entered the program, and he seems to feel more confident and secure with transfers.

Sometimes a patient is referred for evaluation because of a balance dysfunction or recent history of falls. An exercise program may not be indicated. Yet the physical therapist can intervene with recommendations for environmental changes or advise caregivers on safety measures.

Rose W

Rose is 73 years of age. She has been a resident of the long-term care unit for 5 years. She has worked at an ice cream factory, as a homemaker, and as a mother. Rose is married and has three children. Her medical diagnoses include Alzheimer's disease, atherosclerotic heart disease with mitral valve insufficiency, kyphosis, vision problems, and a healed fracture-dislocation of the right shoulder. Rose has been referred to physical therapy following several falls.

At evaluation, Rose could talk, but her speech was largely unintelligible. She was unable to provide a history of her gait or balance difficulties. According to the nurses, Rose often was found on the floor, but it was unclear if she had fallen. Rose had been observed trying to climb on furniture or on the toilet. She had a healing laceration over her right eye.

Rose's functioning was evaluated over 3 days. She was completely uncooperative twice and provided minimal cooperation on the third attempt. ROM was within functional limits. Rose transferred and walked independently; her gait was within normal limits for her age. Rose could maintain standing balance on either foot with one-handed support for 10 seconds. Balance was momentary only on either foot without support. Rose could take several steps backward and could pick up a light object from the floor. Rose would not cooperate with a FR test of balance or mobility performance scale (MPS) testing. She was unable to follow instruction for strength evaluation, although she did not exhibit weakness. Rose was quite agitated; she used quick, repetitive movements and seemed very impatient with testing.

Rose often was found walking without her shoes or with her shoes untied. She sometimes did not wear her glasses. Visual acuity was 20/200 in both eyes. Rose was often agitated and walked around waving her arms wildly and muttering to herself.

Because of her behavior, Rose is at moderate risk for falls. The therapist suggested to nursing that they make sure Rose had her shoes and glasses on properly. To make her totally safe would have required restraining her, either physically or with medication, thus restricting her freedom.

BALANCE TESTING

Impaired balance (also multifactorial) is one cause of instability. Measuring a person's balance is important in assessing risk for falls and provides an objective measurement of improvement in response to treatment.

The FR test,[17,18] is easy to administer and practical and correlates with other measurements of change. It requires less than 5 minutes to administer, including patient instruction and scoring. For this test, attach a yardstick horizontally to the wall. The person stands with her dominant shoulder flexed to 90 degrees and parallel to the yardstick (Figure 8–1). Instruct the patient to reach as far forward as possible without taking a step or leaning against the wall (Figure 8–2).

The FR test is predictive of instability and falls. A person with a FR less than 6 inches has a risk of falling that is eight times greater than that of a person with a FR of more than 10 inches. A person with a reach of 6 to 10 inches has a four times greater than average risk for falls. The test does require the person to stand for 1 minute unsupported. It also requires her to adequately follow instructions. Some patients either cannot stand independently long enough or cannot follow the instructions well enough for testing.

Functional Reach
Subjects must be able to stand for at least 1 minute without any type of assistance
Allow two practice trials and then perform three test trials. Distances reached are averaged
Dominant Hand

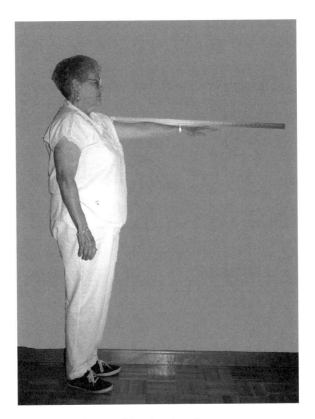

Figure 8–1   Starting position for test of functional reach.

	Start position	*Finish Position*	*Distance Reached (inches)*
Trial 1:	_____	_____	_____
Trial 2:	_____	_____	_____
Trial 3:	_____	_____	_____
Trial 4:	_____	_____	_____
Trial 5:	_____	_____	_____

SLS can be used for balance assessment. This test requires some elements of gait, including single-limb balance and rapid recruitment of muscles, especially around the ankle.[19] In a comparison of elderly adults—one group with and another without a history of falls—there was a significant difference in performance on the SLS test for balance. The study suggested that static balance may be a factor contributing to the incidence of falls in the elderly.[5]

In my experience, the one-foot static standing balance test can be helpful

Figure 8–2 Position of maximal reach on the test.

in determining the appropriate type of assistive device. A person who can maintain balance on either foot for 10 seconds without support does not usually need an assistive device. If he can do so with one-handed support, he can use a cane. If he needs two-handed support to maintain one-foot standing balance, he most likely needs a walker. If a person is unable to balance on either foot for 10 seconds with two-handed support, he probably will not become independent with any assistive device. This test is fairly easy to administer even to a confused person. The instructions can be demonstrated as well as explained.

Other tests used to evaluate balance include the clinical test of sensory interaction and balance,[20] postural stress test,[21,22] and the Berg balance scale.[23]

MOBILITY TESTING

Functional performance in motor tasks represents the sum of a person's abilities in balance, strength, posture, ROM, and sensation. Subtle losses in several areas can add up to a decline in function and an increased risk for falls.[15]

Mobility testing is the best single predictor of recurrent falling. It is simple, yet it recreates complex fall situations and provides a dynamic, integrated assessment of mobility.[24]

Functional mobility can be assessed with various tests that measure performance. These include the timed get up and go test (Mathias),[25,26] the performance-oriented mobility assessment (Tinetti),[24] the functional independence measure (FIM),[27] and the MPS.[28]

The MPS[28] takes only 5 to 10 minutes to administer and requires little equipment. It is hierarchial in that those who can perform the most difficult tasks can also perform the easier ones. The clinician can begin testing at the middle of the scale and, depending on the person's ability to perform the task, test items that are easier or more difficult. Scale scores range from 0 to 7. In a study of 69 older people, this scale discriminated non-fallers from one-time fallers and repeated fallers. The median score for non-fallers was 6, for one-time fallers 5, and for repeated fallers 2.5.[28]

Mobility Performance Scale

Equipment: straight-backed, hard-seated chair, 12-inch ruler, pencil

Sitting Balance
Have the patient sit in a conventional straight-backed kitchen-type chair and ask, "Will you sit forward in the chair, arms folded across your chest, for 1 minute?"

1 = Can sit upright unsupported for 60 seconds
0 = Cannot sit upright independently for 60 seconds (slumps forward or
    to the side)

_____

Sitting Reach
Hold a ruler 12 inches beyond the patient's dominant hand reach and ask "Will you reach forward and get this ruler out of my hand?"

1 = Reaches forward and successfully grasps ruler
0 = Cannot grasp, requires arm support, or does not reach

_____

Picking Up Object from the Floor
With patient standing, drop a pencil in front of the patient within his or her base of support. Ask, "Will you pick up this pencil from the floor?"

1 = Performs independently (without help from object or person)
0 = Performs with some help or support or is unable to pick up object
    and return to standing

_____

Standing Reach

With patient standing, hold a ruler 12 inches beyond patient's dominant-hand reach in such a way that reaching requires a 45-degree plane forward motion. Ask, "Will you reach forward and get this ruler from me?"

1 = Reaches forward and successfully grasps ruler without stepping or holding on

0 = Reaches forward but cannot grasp ruler without stepping or holding on or does not reach

———

Rising from a Chair

Have the patient sit in a conventional straight-backed kitchen-type chair with his or her arms folded across the chest or held out in front. Ask, "Will you get up from the chair without using your arms to push up?"

1 = Done easily on first try

0 = Not done easily on first try

———

Walking

Measure a 10-foot pathway. Indicate the distance to the patient and allow a 3- to 5-foot warm-up. Ask, "Will you walk in your usual way from here to here?"

1 = Stable, safe gait

0 = Unstable, can't do without an assistive device (requires intervention to keep from falling or staggers, trips)

———

Stairs

Ask, "Will you go down these stairs in your usual way?"

1 = Steady, may use railing

0 = Unsteady, can't do

———

Preferred assistive device used during activities:

———— Wheelchair

———— Walker (regular or wheeled)

———— Quad cane (wide or narrow base)

_____ Straight cane

_____ Other _____

_____ None

The timed get up and go test[25,26] is easy to use and requires little equipment. To take the test, the patient sits in a standard chair with arm rests, stands up, walks 3 meters (3.3 yards), turns around, walks 3 meters back to the chair, turns around, and sits back down. The time required to perform the task is measured in seconds.

No one test of balance or function is applicable to all patients and environments.[29] Including the tasks of rolling and transfers in and out of bed should improve the usefulness of these tests for people with more severe functional impairments. It is important for the clinician to consider applicability to the specific patient population, speed and ease of administration, and equipment needed.[29]

Balance and mobility tests are important features of a complete evaluation of an elderly patient by a physical therapist. The tests are reliable and valid for quantifying functional mobility and are useful in measuring clinical change over time. The tests evaluate well-recognized maneuvers in everyday life and correlate well with other measures of balance, speed, and functional abilities.

ENVIRONMENTAL ASSESSMENT

Studies have shown that the most likely site for falls in nursing homes is the bedside. The second most likely place is corridors.[4] Evaluation of a person's safety in her environment must be done with the person present. Merely asking about the environment is not satisfactory. Many older people do not mention difficulties in an attempt to appear more independent than they are.[16]

It is absolutely necessary to evaluate the environment with the patient while she performs her usual activities of daily living. For example, you may find a short patient cannot use a high toilet seat safely. Another patient who cannot reach his shoes because they are under the bed could use a shoe rack.

Building Accessibility   Walk with the patient to the main building entrance. The angle of the ramp should not begin at the door. There should be a level area to allow a wheelchair user to stop to open the door (or have it opened for him) without rolling backward. The door should not be too heavy for the person to open.

Hallways   Halls should be carpeted or tiled; if tiled, a nonskid wax should be used. The floor should not be too reflective to avoid glare or have confusing patterns. Hallway rails in a contrasting color to the wall are a good idea.

Water fountains should be accessible to both a person who is standing and people in wheelchairs. Round doorknobs are often difficult to open; a lever type is easier for a person with arthritis.

Lighting Impaired vision is an important reason for falls in nursing homes.[11] Older people require three times more light than younger people to facilitate vision. However, it may not always be beneficial to simply increase the lighting. People with cataracts may not be able to tolerate bright lighting, especially glare.[16] Assess a person's vision (with glasses on) by having her walk through her environment. Lighting at night is especially important.

Bedrooms Walk with the patient to his room and ask him to carry out normal activities of daily living. Light switches and call bells should be accessible to the patient. The patient should be able to reach his own clothing and personal items in cabinets and drawers. The patient's bed should have locking wheels or no wheels. The patient should be able to sit on his bed with his feet firmly planted on the floor.

An electric high-low bed is preferable to a fixed bed. The low position improves the safety of transfers, and the high position makes it easier for the staff to change the linen. Full side rails on the bed are sometimes used to keep the person in bed. However, if the person is determined enough, he will try to climb over them. Half side rails are preferable for the person who can transfer and walk independently. For a person with a visual problem, a brightly colored target bedspread or seat cushion on a wheelchair may assist transfers.

Clothing Assess the person's clothing for ability to allow the person to dress and undress independently. Tiny buttons, back zippers, and high necks may be impossible. Men's trousers with button and zipper closures are often difficult. They require two hands to manage, which necessitates good balance in standing. If fastened sitting down, the pants can be too loose when the person stands. Pants with elastic waist bands may be preferable. If a person is continent (or could become so if assisted to the bathroom at intervals) his clothing is especially important. The type of incontinence pad with side tape closures or snaps is difficult for patients to manage alone. Bathrobes should not be longer than ankle length to avoid trips.

The type of shoe the person wears is especially important. Scuffs, platform shoes, high heels, shoes with slippery soles, and some types of slip-on shoes are not appropriate. The person should be able to don and doff her shoes; loafers, elastic shoelaces, or a long-handled shoe horn may be needed.

Dining Room, Day Room Ask the person to sit in the chair he generally uses. He should sit comfortably with his feet flat on the floor, and his knees should be flexed to not more than 90 degrees. Armrests on chairs assist transfers. The armrests should fit under the table. Some elderly people put a hand on the back of a chair for support when maneuvering around it, or on the edge of a table when arising to stand. Chairs and tables should be stable when leaned on.

Bathrooms Accompany the person to the bathroom. Wheelchair users need grab bars on one side of the toilet only. Grab bars on both sides can actually block accessibility. For many people, the toilet seat should be elevated. Sink, soap dispenser, and paper towel dispenser should be low enough for wheelchair users. People who have urinary urgency or disorientation at night should be encouraged to use a bedside commode.[2]

Bathing Facilities The shower stall should have a flat threshold. Well-located grab bars in a contrasting color to the wall help transfers. Much equipment is available for people with impaired mobility. The devices include shower seats with swingaway, removable footrests and armrests; tub seats; tub transfer seats; hydraulic seats; patient-lifting devices (Hoyer lifts); and hand-held showers. Evaluate the person's needs for the safest and most appropriate system. Bathing equipment may be expensive, but it is ultimately cheaper than a patient or staff (lifting) injury.

FALL RISK ASSESSMENT

When asked about falls during an interview, elderly people often do not recall them accurately.[30] They may feel demeaned by any admission of weakness or resent reminders that they are no longer as capable as when they were younger. When pressed about the reason for a fall, a patient may say he tripped or was pushed. The person may fear admission of dizziness or weakness may result in his being placed in a vest restraint "for his own good" or that some activities will be limited. Quiet, nonjudgmental reassurance allows the person to be forthright about the circumstances of a fall.

    Name
    History: Describe most recent fall or falls in detail
        Syncope or seizure history
        Medications, especially recent changes
        Recent change in cognition or functional ability
    Acute medical problems
    Clinical evaluation
        ROM limitations
        Strength limitations
        Vertebral artery test, positional vital signs
        Sensory deficits (vision, hearing, tactile); devices used
        Balance testing—FR, SLS, postural stress test
    Adaptive equipment used—bed, wheelchair, bedside commode
    Functional assessment—MPS, get up and go test
    Amount of supervision or assistance required
        Bed mobility

Supine to sitting
Sitting to supine
Rolling to right or left
Transfers
Sitting to standing
Standing to sitting
Time required to execute
Ambulation
On level
On steps
Assistive device recommended
Time required to walk from bed to bathroom, or 15 feet
Bathing
Recommended equipment
Amount of assistance required
Specify independent, far supervision, close supervision, contact guarding, minimal assistance, moderate assistance, maximal assistance, dependent
Recommendations
Clothing, shoes
Equipment
Environmental
Other
Overall fall risk assessment

RESTRAINTS

Studies have shown that mechanical restraints are commonly used in nursing homes. Although the prevalence is not well-documented,[31] various estimates are that 32 to 85 percent of nursing home patients are restrained at some time.[31-35] The number of patients who are restrained at any time is generally underreported in nursing facilities.[36]

Reasons for the use of restraints are often not documented in charts.[32] Nurses report that preventing falls, disruptive behavior such as agitation, and wandering are the common reasons.[33,34,36]

What Types of Restraints Are Used in Nursing Homes?

Restraints can be divided into physical and chemical (drug) types and are used for different purposes. Physical restraints include vest restraints, often called Poseys, after the name of a manufacturer. Vests or waist belts are used in a chair or bed, often to prevent the person from getting up unattended.

Wrist restraints help prevent a person from pulling out a urinary indwelling catheter, nasogastric tube, or intravenous line. All three devices, although sometimes necessary in the short term, are often annoying to the patient and pose risks. Urinary catheters can lead to bladder infections if left in place too long. They can also cause the person to trip while walking. Nasogastric tubes are uncomfortable and cosmetically unappealing and can cause irritation and erosion of nasal passages. Intravenous lines can interfere with functional use of the hands. There are alternatives to the long-term use of these devices. A bladder control program can be used for incontinence. Intermittent catheterization can replace an indwelling catheter for a neurogenic bladder. A gastric feeding tube can replace a nasogastric tube. Medications can often be administered by mouth or by intramuscular injection rather than intravenously. Enteral tube feeding can replace parenteral nutrition through an intravenous line for patients unable to swallow.

Full side rails on the bed are used to keep patients from climbing out of bed. Unfortunately, a determined person can usually defeat them by climbing over the rails, which is even more dangerous than falling out of bed. For a person who can transfer and walk independently, half rails are a safe substitute. For independent or supervised transfers, the person can use half rails to assist in pulling up from supine to sitting.

Other physical restraints include a wheelchair seat belt (if the person cannot unfasten it), wheelchair brakes (if the person cannot reach them), and wheelchair trays. A reclined geriatric chair, with or without a tray, is a less obvious form of restraint.

Chemicals (drugs) can restrain a person by sedating him, making him too lethargic to move. Often, this is a side effect of a drug prescribed for other purposes. Medications are also used to sedate a person before blood work, injections, or medical tests. Medications are also used deliberately to control a patient who is loud and disruptive. However, studies have shown that elderly people who take psychotropic drugs have a greater risk of falling than patients who do not take such drugs.[10,31]

What Are the Consequences of Restraints?

Patient reactions include anger, fear, resistance, humiliation, and demoralization.[31,32,37] The use of restraints may contribute to cognitive decline.[31,38,39] Physical effects include skin breakdown, urinary retention, and aspiration.[31] In addition, some studies suggest that mechanical restraints are not effective in preventing falls[40] and may even increase the risk of injuries.[35] Furthermore, vest and restraint straps have been found to be an underrecognized and underreported cause of death in at least 1 of every 1000 nursing home deaths.[41]

There is a tendency by institutions to rely on restraints to compensate for staff shortages and increased health care costs.[31] In a study of nurses' attitudes toward restraints, 65% could think of no alternative to restraining patients. Among the rest, the most frequent alternative mentioned was to "increase staff."[36] However, the opposite is true—larger nursing staffs correlated with increased use of restraints.[34]

What Are Alternatives to the Use of Restraints?

There are practical, safe, and humane alternatives to use of restraints. Instead of having his freedom limited, perhaps a patient can be assisted to become more independent in mobility by using a wheelchair or can be allowed to walk with supervision. If he is kept awake by interesting activities during the day, maybe the patient will sleep better at night with less tendency to roam.

If a restraint must be used, some are less restrictive than others. A seat belt, if the person can release it independently, is less restrictive than a vest or waist-belt restraint. For a person who tends to slide forward and off the chair, a wedge seat cushion can improve sitting posture. A person who lacks enough trunk control to sit erect can use a reclined wheelchair to improve posture. The primary reason for these devices is comfortable positioning, but the devices have the additional advantage of discouraging patients from getting up unattended.

A patient who is able to walk and apt to get up at night should have the bed fairly low to the floor and without full side rails.

For the patient who is unsteady walking, alternatives to restraints include an alarm system attached to bed, chair, or patient to alert caregivers when the person sits up and attempts to get out of the bed or chair unattended.

As an alternative to wrist restraints, mittens can be used in the short term. Mittens are restraint devices, but they are less uncomfortable and less restrictive than wrist restraints.

Restraints are used to prevent a confused person from wandering. Alternatives include exit and stairwell alarms. An individual electronic device, worn on the wrist, can be placed on patients likely to wander. Sensors are placed at doors that activate an alarm when the resident tries to pass through. In this way, exits can be controlled without restricting the free movement of staff and visitors.

SUPPLIERS

Bed and Chair Alarms

TABS Mobility Monitor
Wanderguard Inc.
P. O. Box 80238
Lincoln, NE 68501
800-824-2996

Code Alert Bed/Chair Alarm
RF Technologies, Inc.
3720 North 124th Street
Milwaukee, WI 53222
800-669-9946

Chair Sentinel (releasing seat belt causes an audible tone)
Powderhorn Industries
931 N Park Ave
P.O. Box 1443
Montrose, CO 81402
800-336-1414

Perimeter Systems

WanderGuard Monitoring System
Wanderguard, Inc.
P.O. Box 80238
Lincoln, NE 68501
800-824-2996

Code Alert System
RF Technologies, Inc.
Smart Guard Alarm Systems
800-234-0683

Saf-T-Lok
10028 S Western Ave
Chicago, IL 60643
800-643-0680

CASE REPORTS

The following case reports describe two patients who, through a combination of a maintenance exercise program and coordination with nursing, were able to discontinue use of restraints.

Angelina D

Angelina is 72 years of age, the daughter of an Italian family from South Philadelphia. She was not educated and is illiterate, but is not unintelligent. She was married just before her 15th birthday to a man from the neighborhood who was 30 years her senior. Together they raised five children. Eighteen years ago, Angelina's youngest son died at the age of 22 of a drug overdose. Angelina became severely depressed and medical problems developed that necessitated several abdominal operations. Angelina withdrew from her family and became addicted to Percodan (oxycodone). Ten years ago Angelina was admitted to a psychiatric hospital. Because her cognitive status declined, Angelina was admitted to a long-term care unit 2 years later. Her husband died 15 years ago. Her son Vincent visits two to three times a week, and the other children also visit from time to time.

Angelina's medical history includes a left modified radical mastectomy 2 years ago. She fell 7 years ago, sustaining a fracture of the fifth metacarpal of the right hand, and again 3 years ago, sustaining fractures of the right third and fourth metatarsals. The fractures healed well, and Angelina resumed independent transfers and ambulation without an assistive device. Six months ago a urinary tract infection developed, and a catheter was inserted. For 3 weeks Angelina was placed in a geriatric chair with a tray to prevent her from getting up or removing the catheter. The catheter was removed, and Angelina was referred to physical therapy to begin walking again.

At evaluation, Angelina was nonverbal, except for repeated requests for soda water. At 5 feet 4 inches and 172 pounds, Angelina was obese, with a protuberant abdomen. Notable was facial dyskinesia with almost continual tongue thrusting, decreased control of respirations, and gasping. Her feet were pronated left greater than right. Other ROM was within normal limits for age. The therapist was unable to perform specific tests of strength because of Angelina's cognitive deficits, but strength appeared functionally intact.

Angelina could transfer with close supervision; however, she sought assistance to stand, especially if touched. She could walk 100 feet with close supervision. She walked with short steps and a wide base of support, with her lower extremities in external rotation of 40 degrees and decreased trunk rotation. Angelina had difficulty with weight-shifting, noted during transfers and turning.

She was unable to follow instructions for either the FR or SLS tests of balance. Angelina scored 3/7 on the MPS. Her other problems included inattentiveness and shortness of breath during ambulation and poor endurance.

Angelina began participation in a group ambulation and exercise program to maintain and improve her endurance and safety. She could participate in most activities. However, her attention span was very limited, with frequent restless movements of her head and extremities. For example, Angelina seemed unable to stand still in one place but walked forward, glancing around frantically. She had trouble focusing on tasks. Asked to throw a ball or a beanbag, Angelina did not gaze at the target but glanced at it and then turned away while throwing. Despite this behavior, Angelina was generally cooperative. She continued to require contact guarding for transfers and ambulation.

Two months ago, Angelina was hospitalized with unstable diabetes and a urinary tract infection. Back from the hospital, Angelina was noticeably thinner, especially in her face and limbs. She was generally debilitated, and her standing balance had declined. The therapist began to work with Angelina on an individual basis, first in the parallel bars and then with contact guarding as previously. In 3 weeks, Angelina's overall functional status had improved to the level before hospitalization. Her endurance generally improved and she could walk more than 100 feet without shortness of breath. She became calmer and no longer hyperventilated.

Angelina has returned to the group program. She remains at risk for falls, especially during transfers, because of her dyskinesia and inattention. Angelina is especially unsteady when first getting up from a chair, and she sometimes attempts to get up unattended. However, Angelina is unhappy when restrained and often becomes agitated. Despite the risk, the therapist recommended Angelina's restraints be discontinued.

Curtis C

Curtis is 73 years of age. He has been a resident of a long-term care facility for 5 years. He has an 11th grade education and has worked in a shoe factory. He is married and has children; the family visits regularly. Diagnoses include organic brain syndrome and seizure disorder.

Curtis was completely independent with all transfers and ambulation until 8 months ago. An increase in seizure activity was noticed, as was unsteadiness walking and several falls and near-falls. Curtis was hospitalized with a seizure disorder, left cerebral vascular accident (right hemiplegia), and pneumonia. He returned to the long-term care facility 1 week later.

At evaluation, Curtis was largely nonverbal, but he responded with short phrases (eg, "feel OK") or by nodding his head. He was lethargic. ROM was full. Curtis could move all extremities, but coordination was impaired and he frequently postured his hands and wrists. Curtis was tactile defensive and would splay his fingers, actively avoiding using his hands whenever he could. Muscle strength could not be tested because Curtis was unable to follow instructions.

Transfers sitting to standing required moderate assistance. Curtis had a shuffling gait with a tendency to lose his balance, especially forward. Curtis could walk up to 50 feet with contact guarding and frequent balance assistance of two. The only sign of hemiplegia was in standing balance. With one-handed support Curtis could maintain his balance on his left foot for 5 seconds and on his right only momentarily. Because of the severe risk of falls, Curtis was restrained in a chair on the unit.

The therapist worked with Curtis on improving his balance and transfers and use of a wheeled walker. When arising from a chair, Curtis clasped his hands together and did not use them appropriately to push up from the chair. He sometimes rocked backward and forward four or five times before attaining standing balance. Walking with the walker, Curtis would sometimes still require balance assistance. He also tended to push the walker too far ahead of him.

Nevertheless, Curtis did respond to verbal and physical cues and made slow but steady progress. In 6 weeks, he required only close supervision for transfers. Use of the walker was discontinued, and Curtis became fully ambulatory without an assistive device. SLS was 8 seconds on either foot with one-handed support. Curtis was unable to follow instructions for a FR test. He scored 6/7 on the MPS. Curtis did have some gait abnormalities, but these were consistent with his gait before hospitalization. Stance was wide-based with excessive lateral weight shift and decreased trunk rotation. Curtis usually walked with his hands clasped together or put them in his pockets, although he put them to his side for 15 to 30 seconds when cued to do so. Curtis had not had any falls since his hospitalization and could be considered safe walking independently indoors on level surfaces. Use of restraints was discontinued.

Curtis was discharged from physical therapy and was ready to participate in group exercises. Goals of his maintenance program are to increase the amount of independent ambulation on the unit, improve the safety of his gait, and encourage appropriate use of his hands. Over the last 6 months, Curtis's functional status has remained unchanged. He has become more active and now spends most of the day walking around. He has not had any seizures or falls.

FALLS, RESTRAINTS, AND MOBILITY

In a study of nursing attitudes, falling is cited as significantly more important than all other reasons for the use of restraints. Unfortunately, nurses do generally have a positive attitude toward the use of restraints.[36]

Nurses' concerns about legal liability seem to encourage use of restraints.[31,36] Studies show that nurses commonly believe that when they are following orders to restrain a patient, they are on safe legal ground. If nurses have an order to restrain as needed for a patient's safety and a patient breaks a hip while not restrained, nurses often believe they can be held liable.[31] However, if restraints are applied continuously and the patient loses the ability to walk, neither the physician nor nurse is held accountable for the patient's loss of mobility.[31] In a recent study, only 42 percent of nurses believed they would receive administrative support if an unrestrained patient fell.[36] It has been shown that an educational program aimed at altering staff beliefs and increasing knowledge about restraints can produce a change in practices, at least in the short term.[42]

Falls are also an important liability concern for facilities. Two important causes of insurance claims are resident falls and wandering. Resident falls alone account for 67 percent of claims filed against facilities.[43] In response to these concerns, facilities have developed standardized procedures that are expected to be followed in case of a fall. The first question is defining when a fall has occurred. If a patient is found on the floor, should it be assumed she has fallen? Some patients deliberately sit on the floor. Staff members often define a fall as occurring only if there is an obvious injury. If a staff person safely lowers a person who is slipping to the floor, is this a fall?

Procedure generally includes the completion of an incident report, which is often time-consuming. In addition, the incident report may be used to assign blame for the fall. It is not surprising that incident reports are often not completed unless there has been an injury. A higher incidence of falls is discovered by a chart review than with review of incident reports." Perhaps there is too much emphasis on the "incident," ignoring the degree of injury or the circumstances. This emphasis may increase staff use of restraints. An efficient, nonjudgmental system should be used for reporting falls.[44]

A person with little mobility (eg, someone who must stay in bed) has little risk of falls. A person who transfers and walks independently without impairments is also unlikely to fall. Paradoxically, by helping a patient improve functional mobility, the therapist may increase the risk for falls,[8] as shown in Figure 8–3.

The benefits of greater independence and self esteem often justify interventions to improve mobility. These benefits may outweigh to a patient, family, and caregivers the possible increased risk of falls.

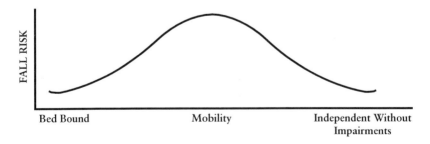

Figure 8–3   Risk of falls related to degree of mobility.

SUMMARY

Falls and resulting injuries are a serious problem for the elderly, especially those in institutions. Efforts to prevent falls often lead to the sometimes inappropriate use of restraints and eventual loss of mobility. The application of restraints is usually a nursing rather than a medical decision.[45] However, the decision to use any type of restraint should include all members of the health care team.

Depriving a person of his autonomy and ability to control his own body and movements is serious and may result in unforeseen consequences. All possible alternatives should be explored. If it is decided that restraints must be used, the patient and her family should be consulted about the type of restraint, length of time it is used, circumstances, and reason for use.

It is impossible to prevent all falls. However, a well-planned program can reduce the risks of injurious falls while promoting autonomy, dignity, and independence.

RECOMMENDATIONS

1. All patients' risk for falls should be periodically assessed.
2. The decision to use restraints should include all care team members, including physical therapists.
3. A prevention program of ambulation and exercise is indicated for people at risk for falls or loss of mobility.

REFERENCES

1. Cutson TM. Falls in the elderly. *Am Fam Physician* 1994;49:149–156.
2. Daleiden S. Clinical implications of neurologic changes in the aging process. In: Lewis CB, ed. *Aging: The health care challenge,* 2d ed. Philadelphia: Davis, 1990, pp. 162–180.
3. Brady R, Chester FR, Pierce LL, Salter JP, Schreck S, Radziewicz R. Geriatric falls: Prevention strategies for the staff. *J Gerontol Nurs* 1993;19:26–32.
4. Rhymes J, Jaeger R. Falls: Prevention and management in the institutional setting. *Clin Geriatr Med* 1988;1:613–622.
5. Gehlsen GM Whaley MH. Falls in the elderly. II. Balance, strength and flexibility. *Arch Phys Med Rehabil* 1990;71:739–741.
6. Ryynanen OP, Kivela SL, Honkanen R, Laippala P, Soini P. Incidence of falling injuries leading to medical treatment in the elderly. *Public Health* 1991;105:373–386.
7. Myers AH, Baker SP, Van Natta ML, Abbey H, Robinson EG. Risk factors associated with falls and injuries among elderly institutionalized persons. *Am J Epidemiol* 1991;133:1179–1190.
8. Svensson ML, Rundgren A, Larsson M, Oden A, Sund V, Landahl S. Accidents in the institutionalized elderly: A risk analysis. *Aging* 1991;3:181–192.
9. Ray WA. Psychotropic drugs and injuries among the elderly: A review. *J Clin Psychopharmacol* 1992;12:382–383.

10. Arfken CL, Birge SJ, Miller JP. Maladaptive behavior: A risk factor for falls resulting from slips and trips. *J Am Geriatr Soc* 1991;39:A10.

11. Jantti PO, Pyykko VI, Hervonen AL. Falls among elderly nursing home residents. *Public Health* 1993;107:89–96.

12. Roberts BL, Wykle ML. Pilot study results: Falls among institutionalized elderly. *J Gerontol Nurs* 1993;19:13–20.

13. Clark RD, Lord SR, Webster IW. Clinical parameters associated with falls in an elderly population. *Gerontology* 1993;39:117–123.

14. Tinetti ME. Instability and falling in elderly patients. *Semin Neurol* 1989;9:39–45.

15. Duncan PW, Chandler J, Studenski S, Hughes M, Prescott B. How do physiological components of balance affect mobility in elderly men? *Arch Phys Med Rehabil* 1993;74:1343–1349.

16. Tideiksaar R. *Falling in old age: Its prevention and treatment.* New York: Springer Publishing, 1989.

17. Weiner DK, Duncan PW, Chandler J, Studenski SA. Functional reach: A marker of physical frailty. *J Am Geriatr Soc* 1992;10:203–207.

18. Duncan P, Weiner DK, Chandler J, Studenski S. Functional reach: A new clinical measure of balance. *J Gerontol* 1990:45:M192–M197.

19. Tropp H, Odenrick P. Postural control in single limb stance. *J Orthop Res* 1988;6:833–839.

20. Cohen H, Blatchly CA, Gombash, LL. A study of the clinical test of sensory interaction and balance. *Phys Ther* 1993;73:346–350.

21. Chandler JM, Duncan PW, Studenski SA. Balance performance on the postural stress test: Comparison of young adults, healthy elderly, and fallers. *Phys Ther* 1990;70:410–415.

22. Wolfson LI, Whipple R, Amerman P, Kleinberg A. Stressing the postural response: A quantitative method for testing balance. *J Am Geriatr Soc* 1986;34:845–850.

23. Berg K, Wood-Dauphinee S, Williams J, Gayton D. Measuring balance in the elderly: Preliminary development of an instrument. *Physiother Can* 1989;41:304–308.

24. Tinetti ME. Performance-oriented assessment of mobility problems in elderly patients. *J Am Geriatr Soc* 1986;34:119–126.

25. Mathias S, Nayak U, Isaacs B. Balance in elderly patients: The get-up and go test. *Arch Phys Med Rehabil* 1986;67:387–389.

26. Podsiadlo D, Richardson S. The timed "up & go": A test of basic functional mobility for frail elderly persons. *J Am Geriatr Soc* 1991;39:142–148.

27. Linacre JM, Heinemann AW, Wright BD, Granger CV, Hamilton BB. The structure and stability of the functional independence measure. *Arch Phys Med Rehabil* 1994:75:127–132.

28. Hogue CC, Studenski S, Duncan P. Assessing mobility: The first step in falls prevention. In: Funk SG, Tornquist EM, Champagne MP, Copp LA, Weise RA, eds. *Key aspects of recovery: Improving nutrition, rest and mobility.* New York: Springer Publishing, 1990, pp. 275–280.

29. Duncan PW, Shumway-Cook A, Tinetti ME, Whipple RH, Wolf S, Woollacott M: Is there one simple measure for balance?: *PT Mag Phys Ther* January 1993:74–81.

30. Cummings SR, Nevitt MC, Kidd S. Forgetting falls: The limited accuracy of recall of falls in the elderly. *J Am Geriatr Soc* 1988;36:613–616.

31. Conely LG, Campbell LA. The use of restraints in caring for the elderly: Realities, consequences and alternatives. *Nurse Pract* 1991;16(12):48, 51–52.

32. Marks W. Physical restraints in the practice of medicine: Current concepts. *Arch Intern Med* 1992;152:2203–2206.

33. Tinetti ME, Liu WL, Marottoli RA, Ginter SF. Mechanical restraint use among residents of skilled nursing facilities. Prevalence, patterns and predictors. *JAMA* 1991;265:168–171.

34. Magee R, Hyatt EC, Hardin SB, Stratmann D, Vinson MH, Owen M. Institutional policy: Use of restraints in extended care and nursing homes. *J Gerontol Nurs* 1993;19(4):31–39.

35. Tinetti ME, Liu WL, Ginter SF. Mechanical restraint use and fall-related injuries among residents of skilled nursing facilities. *Ann Intern Med* 1992;116:369–374.

36. Hardin SB, Magee, R, Stratmann, D, Vinson MH, Owen M, Hyatt EC. Extended care and nursing home staff attitudes toward restraints. *J Gerontol Nurs* 1994;20(3):23–31.

37. Eigsti DG, Vrooman N. Releasing restraints in the nursing home: It can be done. *J Gerontol Nurs* 1992;18(1):21–23.

38. Kane RL, Williams CC, Williams TF, Kane, RA. Restraining restraints: Changes in a standard of care. *Annu Rev Public Health* 1993;14:545–584.

39. Burton LC, German PS, Rovner BW, Brant LJ. Physical restraint use and cognitive decline among nursing home residents. *J Am Geriatr Soc* 1992;40:811–816.

40. Ginter SF, Mion LC. Falls in the nursing home: Preventable or inevitable? *J Gerontol Nurs* 1992;18(11):43–48.

41. Miles SH, Irvine P. Deaths caused by physical restraints. *Gerontologist* 1992;32:762–766.

42. Strumpf NE, Evans LK, Wagner J, Patterson J. Reducing physical restraints: Developing an educational program. *J Gerontol Nurs* 1992;18(11):21–27.

43. Foxwell, L. Risk management decreases incidence of falls, wandering. *Provider* 1993;October:51.

44. Kanten DN, Mulrow CD, Geraty MB, Lichtenstein MJ, Aguilar C, Cornall JE. Falls: An evaluation of three reporting methods in nursing homes. *J Am Geriatr Soc* 1993;41:662–666.

45. Schleenbaker RE, McDowell SM, Moore RW, Costich JF, Prater G. Restraint use in inpatient rehabilitation: Incidence, predictors and implications. *Arch Phys Med Rehabil* 1994;75:427–430.

9

Administration and Total Quality Management

VALUE OF A PREVENTION PROGRAM

Individual Patient Benefits of a Prevention Program
- Maintaining muscle strength, range of motion, endurance
- Independent mobility—ambulation or wheelchair
- Independence in self care
- Injury prevention
- Preserving dignity, self esteem

Facility Benefits of a Prevention Program
- Prevention of patient and staff injuries
- Conserving staff time and resources
- Reduced liability concerns
- Marketing to the community

Reimbursement Issues

Most people would agree that maximizing a patient's independence with activities of daily living saves money and staff time. A program that prevents falls saves health care dollars otherwise spent on hip fractures and other injuries.

Medicare and private insurance cover direct physical therapy for skilled services for only a brief period of time after an acute injury or onset of disease.

However, there is provision for the establishment and monitoring of maintenance programs in the Health Care Financing Administration (HCFA) (Medicare) regulations. Under the regulations in Section 409.00 "(c) Services which would qualify as skilled rehabilitation services.

(5) Maintenance therapy; Maintenance therapy, when the specialized knowledge and judgement of a qualified therapist is required to design and

111

establish a maintenance program based on an initial evaluation and periodic reassessment of the patient's needs, and consistent with the patient's capacity and tolerance. For example, a patient with Parkinson's disease who has not been under a rehabilitation regimen may require the services of a qualified therapist to determine what type of exercise will contribute the most to the maintenance of his present level of functioning."[1]

Group exercise programs implemented under the supervision of a physical therapist meet this definition.[1] In addition, if the participants are drawn from the general population, the therapist can screen for conditions that may be covered under the patients' insurance.

REFERRAL TO PROGRAM

Referral sources include the following

- The initial screening process when a patient is admitted to the facility
- Physician referral, often after a fall or injury
- The nursing department, often for psychosocial benefits
- The therapist of a patient who has completed the rehabilitative phase of recovery from an acute injury or disease
- The patient or a family member who recognizes the need for an ongoing prevention program

Some states, and perhaps more in the future, allow the public direct access to physical therapy services. This legally permits physical therapists to evaluate and treat a patient without a physician's order. However, most states continue to require a written referral. Reimbursement for services is a separate issue. Insurers, including Medicare, require a physician's order for reimbursement of the cost of treatment.

DISCHARGE FROM PROGRAM

Reasons for discharge from the program include the following

- Patient improved and able to maintain functional status without continued intervention
- Consistent patient refusals to participate in treatment
- Hospitalization—readmission requires physical therapy re-evaluation (and physician orders in many states)
- Patient is disruptive to the group (may call for change in patient's program, not necessarily discharge)
- Death

Discharge from the program should occur after consultation with the patient, physician, and nurses.

INTERRUPTIONS IN THE PROGRAM: AVOIDABLE AND NOT

Possible reasons for interruptions in a patient's participation in the program include the following

- Medical appointments
- Illness
- Religious services
- Patient bathing
- Barber, hairdresser
- Administration of medication
- Bathroom needs

Some interruptions can be minimized through timely communication with nurses and others.

PHARMACOLOGIC EFFECTS ON TREATMENT

The physiologic changes that accompany aging can affect the way various medications are metabolized. Medications are converted more slowly in the elderly and exert a more prolonged effect than in younger people. Some drugs, such as phenytoin (Dilantin), may accumulate in the system and can reach toxic levels. In addition, elderly people often take many different drugs, increasing the likelihood of drug interactions. The various symptoms seen in physical therapy may be caused by the primary disease, a side effect or adverse effect of medications taken to treat the disease, or even an overdose of the medication. These effects can be detrimental to the effectiveness and even the safety of physical therapy.[2]

Among the symptoms that directly affect physical therapy are motor and sensory dysfunction, cardiopulmonary effects, and mental and central nervous system (CNS) changes.[3]

Motor and Sensory Dysfunction

Parkinsonism Symptoms of Parkinson's disease include resting tremor, bradykinesia, rigidity, and festinating gait. These symptoms may occur if Parkinson's disease is not treated adequately. Levodopa is often prescribed. The side effects associated with levodopa include cardiac arrhythmia, postural hypotension, dyskinesia, and mood changes. Dopamine agonists, anticholinergic drugs, amantadine (Symmetrel), and deprenyl (Selegiline) also are prescribed for Parkinson's disease and can have similar side effects.

Symptoms of Parkinson's disease can result from antipsychotic medications, including chlorpromazine (Thorazine), haloperidol (Haldol), prochlorperazine (Compazine), molindone (Moban), and loxapine (Loxitane).

Sympatholytic drugs methyldopa and reserpine, used to treat hypertension and arrhythmia, may also cause parkinsonism.

Ataxia Cerebellar disturbances may be caused by a seizure disorder and by the various drugs used to treat seizures; that is, barbiturates, benzodiazepines (Ativan, Valium), phenytoin (Dilantin), and carbamazepine (Tegretol).

Tardive Dyskinesia, Akathisia Tardive dyskinesia (involuntary, fragmented, and rhythmic movements) and akathisia (motor restlessness) are common side effects of most antipsychotic drugs. These drugs, such as trifluoperazine (Stelazine) and Haldol, are used to treat schizophrenia and for treatment of organic brain syndrome and parkinsonism.

Tremor Essential tremor may be idiopathic or may be caused by the foregoing medications, which affect the cerebellum. Tremor is also a side effect of lithium (used to treat manic depression), adrenergic drugs (used to treat hypotension, cardiac decompensation, and chronic obstructive pulmonary disease [COPD]), and tricyclic antidepressants. Withdrawal from narcotic analgesics also can cause tremor.

Muscle Weakness and Wasting Fatigue may be caused by a decrease in fluid volume resulting from diuretics and vasodilators (for hypertension). Insulin and oral hypoglycemic agents may result in weakness caused by a drop in blood sugar. Calcium channel blockers (used to treat angina) and digitalis (used to treat congestive heart failure and COPD) at toxic levels may cause muscle weakness. Sedatives cause CNS disturbances that result in lethargy. Long-term use of corticosteriods causes muscle wasting.

Sensory Effects Some medications may have sensory effects that affect treatment. Aspirin can cause tinnitus; atropine may result in blurred vision; and peripheral neuropathy may occur during cancer chemotherapy.

Cardiopulmonary Effects
Hypotension and postural hypotension Many drugs can cause hypotension—a severe and potentially disabling condition in the elderly. Among them are tricyclic antidepressants (used to treat depression); tranquilizers (for psychotic behavior); antihypertensives; diuretics (for congestive heart failure); nitrates (for angina); narcotic analgesics; antiparkinsonian agents; benzodiazepines (for insomnia and anxiety); and anti-arrhythmics.

Cardiac arrhythmia A common side effect with all anti-arrhythmic drugs is an aggravation of cardiac rhythm disturbances. Digitalis (for congestive heart failure) is also associated with arrhythmia. Diuretics are often associated with electrolyte changes that affect cardiac excitability. Beta-adrenergic drugs and xanthine derivative bronchodilators (used to treat COPD) can cause arrhythmias.

Bradycardia, Tachycardia Calcium channel blockers and beta-blockers (for arrhythmia) can cause bradycardia. Tachycardia may be caused by tricyclic antidepressants.

Mental and Central Nervous System Changes

These symptoms affect a person's ability to participate and benefit from an exercise program.

Depression Drugs associated with depression in the elderly are antihypertensives, anti-inflammatories, antimycobacterials, antiparkinsonians, diuretics, sedative-hypnotics, and vasodilators. However, the drugs used to treat depression are also associated with unfortunate side effects. For example, tricyclics cause sedation and confusion, and alprazolam (Xanax) causes agitation and confusion.

Confusion, Dementia Use of any drug that causes confusion leads to dementia over time. Confusion is a side effect of many medications, including, but not limited to, antiparkinsonians, antidepressants, anti-inflammatories, analgesics, sedative-hypnotics, diuretics, hypoglycemic agents, and beta-blockers.

Vertigo Vertigo may result from an inner ear disturbance (Ménière's disease). It also can result from side effects of anti-hypertensives, analgesics, sedative-hypnotics, cholesterol-lowering drugs, and some antibacterial (streptomycin) and antiviral drugs. Vertigo symptoms can be similar to those seen in postural hypotension.

These symptoms can have a profound effect on a person's ability to participate in and respond to an exercise program. In addition, these effects are often more readily observed by the therapist than by other members of the care team. Other symptoms are usually noted first by nurses or do not have such a direct effect on treatment. These include skin conditions, gastrointestinal disturbances, urinary problems, respiratory infections, or changes in liver or kidney function.

In summary, if symptoms interfere with therapy, consider the possibility of drug effects. If the patient is more able to participate in therapy at certain times during the day because of medication influences, perhaps his exercise program can be scheduled to take this into account. Check the chart and discuss the situation with the physician.

CASE REPORTS

Effects of medication can have a profound effect on treatment. The following case report illustrates a medication problem discovered in therapy.

Atlace T

Atlace is 78 years of age and has long-standing medical problems. Her diagnoses include severe arthritis of both knees and hands, atherosclerotic heart disease, and confusion. She has a cardiac arrhythmia, which is treated with Dilantin (phenytoin). Atlace has not been able to walk independently for about 10 years because of deformity and pain in her knees. It was when Atlace lost the ability to walk that she entered long-term care. Atlace was referred to physical therapy for evaluation.

She had valgus deformities of both knees: left 25 degrees and right 20 degrees. Range of motion (ROM) in knee flexion and extension was full. Bilateral shoulder flexion was 90 degrees. Left elbow flexion was 10 to 120 degrees; bilateral wrist flexion was 40 degrees, and there was ulnar drift of the metacarpophalangeal (MCP) joints. Muscle strength was within normal limits for Atlace's age.

Atlace joined a group of five other patients for a nonambulatory group exercise class for ROM and strengthening exercises. The therapist also brought Atlace to the physical therapy department for therapeutic standing and ambulation in the parallel bars. Goals of therapy were to maintain muscle strength, ROM, and ability to walk.

Six months ago, Atlace became lethargic. Formerly quite alert and eager to participate, she was no longer able to follow instructions. The therapist brought this to the physician's attention. After blood tests, Atlace was hospitalized for 1 week with phenytoin toxicity and bradycardia. Common side effects of phenytoin are drowsiness and confusion.[3]

Upon return from the hospital, Atlace was again alert and responsive but debilitated. She was seen for skilled physical therapy for intensive exercise, transfer, and gait training in the parallel bars to restore her to her level of function before hospitalization. In a week, Atlace was again able to participate in group exercise and could walk in the parallel bars 10 feet two times several times a week.

At times, especially in rainy weather, Atlace has pain in her knees that prevents ambulation. The therapist consulted with her physician, who recommended acetaminophen before therapy. A stronger analgesic was not indicated because of the heart condition. Using moist hot packs before walking also helps. On good days, Atlace can walk 20 feet with a wheeled walker, with some help to maneuver the walker. She scored 2/7 on the mobility performance scale (MPS) (see Chapter 8).

Despite the progress in ambulation, it became apparent that because of knee pain and deformity, this could not be Atlace's primary means of mobility. She was not a candidate for knee replacement because of her age and heart disease. At this time, Atlace spent most of her time fully reclined in a geriatric chair, napping off and on throughout the day.

The therapist began to talk to the nurses about obtaining a wheelchair for Atlace, and ran into considerable resistance. The nurses believed Atlace would surely try to get up and would fall. The nurses suggested Atlace could sit in a wheelchair only with a vest restraint on. Eventually, orders were obtained for a wheelchair. Atlace did not require any particular modifications to a standard chair.

Initially, Atlace sat in the chair for only an hour a day in therapy and then transferred back to a geriatric chair when she returned to the unit. Over a month, the therapist gradually increased the amount of time Atlace sat in the wheelchair and began working with her on propelling the chair and maneuvering it independently. Atlace proved quite adept at propelling the chair with encouragement and cues, despite the arthritis in her hands. She also tolerated sitting in the chair and soon was sitting in it in the morning when the therapist arrived. Atlace showed no tendency to try to get out of the chair, and nursing no longer applied restraints. Furthermore, Atlace remained awake during the day.

Later, the therapist featured Atlace on videotape, maneuvering her chair around independently. She very much enjoyed seeing herself on television. Use of the tape during an in-service training session illustrated to staff how much Atlace could do for herself, and they began to encourage her to propel herself to the dining room for meals. Atlace continues to participate in group exercises and walks in the parallel bars or with a walker twice a week. With encouragement she pushes herself to the physical therapy department.

THE INTERDISCIPLINARY TEAM

Cooperation and coordination with all members of the health care team is vital. This includes nurses, aides, social workers, physicians, administration, and occupational and speech therapists. Each service provides a unique perspective in the development of the care plan. This interdepartmental approach is essential to managed care.

Nurses can ensure that patients are physically ready for therapy by having them dressed, including shoes and incontinence pads when necessary. When needed, nursing can assist the patient to the bathroom before a session. Administration of medications and bathing can be coordinated to not interfere with therapy. Nurses can help prepare patients psychologically for therapy. A simple reminder can make a lot of difference in a patient's willingness to participate.

Nurses should advise the therapist whenever a patient has an illness, especially an infectious disease such as conjunctivitis or an upper respiratory infection. In working with patients in a group, which involves handling equipment that cannot be sterilized, universal precautions cannot be applied. The patient should be temporarily excluded.

Perhaps the most important value of communication with nurses is to ensure carry-over of skills taught and reinforced in therapy. A patient who walks in therapy should also walk with the nurses. All too familiar to most therapists is a patient who walks well during the week but relapses by Monday because she has not walked for 2 days. Nurses can be shown how maximizing patient independence in mobility and self care frees staff for other duties. Staff instruction in ways to reinforce skills can be accomplished with staff in-service training or informal demonstration by working with the patient on the floor rather than "down in therapy."

The social work department can aid in communication with the family and with obtaining equipment—from shoes to wheelchairs.

There is often tension, and sometimes misunderstanding, among various departments. Good communication helps resolve these issues. Also, all members of the team should keep in mind that the patient, as the ultimate consumer, is always first. If the patient's welfare is kept paramount, difficulties in communication can be resolved.

CASE REPORT

Close coordination with the nursing department is often absolutely necessary to help the patient return to independence in ambulation, as illustrated by the following case report.

Dorothy S

Dorothy is 60 years of age. She is a patient at a psychiatric hospital and has transferred to the long-term care unit. Dorothy was first hospitalized 20 years ago for psychiatric problems that included hallucinations and an inability to care for her children. Dorothy had no motor problems and was independent with all ambulation without an assistive device until an injury 14 months ago.

At that time, Dorothy was pushed over a wall by another patient. She sustained a burst fracture of L-1 with bilateral paraparesis. Dorothy underwent laminectomy of L-1 and fusion of T9 to L3 with a Harrington rod and a left iliac crest bone graft. She was placed in a body cast. In 6 weeks, the cast was replaced with a spinal orthosis.

One month later, Dorothy was first referred for physical therapy with "minimal motor function in legs" and given little chance of ever walking again. At that time, her verbalizations were continuous and confused. She was able to follow one-step commands about 50 percent of the time if they were repeated firmly several times. ROM was full but with a decrease in tone of both lower extremities. Sensation could not be adequately assessed because of the cognitive and communication deficits.

Muscle strength on the left was knee extension 2/5, hip flexion 1/5, and ankle dorsiflexion 0/5. On the right, knee extension was 4/5, hip flexion 3–/5, and ankle dorsiflexion 1/5. Dorothy could roll to either side using the bed side rails. Moving from supine to sitting required moderate assistance. Dorothy could stand-pivot transfer with minimal assistance and could maintain standing with right (but not left) knee extension.

Dorothy underwent an individual physical therapy program consisting of transfer training, gait training, and exercise. She showed excellent progress in therapy. In 2 weeks, she could walk with a walker with close supervision, although with a left foot drop.

Then, a week later, Dorothy tried to get out of bed by herself, fell, and sustained a left hip fracture. She was treated with open reduction internal fixation of the left hip. Dorothy resumed physical therapy with weight-bearing as tolerated, continuing to wear the spinal orthosis whenever out of bed. In 1 month, Dorothy was beginning to carry her walker, showing she was ready for a cane. However, the left foot drop persisted. Dorothy's walking was evaluated with a ready-made molded ankle-foot orthosis, which corrected the foot drop nicely.

Dorothy continued to work well in therapy. In 6 more weeks, strength in left dorsiflexion had improved to 3+/5. She could walk without a foot drop, and no longer needed to use the ankle-foot orthosis. She had progressed to independent bed mobility. She required supervision only to transfer and walk with a narrow-based quad cane. She swung or occasionally threw a straight cane. Dorothy had residual weakness of her left lower extremity: knee extension 3/5, hip flexion 2+/5, dorsiflexion 3+/5. At this point, after 4 months of individual therapy, Dorothy entered a maintenance program for group exercise with six other patients who were also ambulatory.

Dorothy cooperated well and enjoyed the program. However, although essentially independent walking for an hour a day in therapy, she depended on her wheelchair on the nursing unit. She was often restrained in the wheelchair, although she was quite independent at that level, maneuvering the chair all around the building. After 2 months, the nurses and the therapist decided to encourage Dorothy to discontinue using the wheelchair. She continued to participate in group exercise every day and then sat in a conventional chair or walked under nursing supervision for gradually longer periods of time each day. Dorothy adjusted well to this routine and was soon walking the halls independently.

Sometimes Dorothy forgot the cane and walked without it. However, this seemed to cause back and hip pain—Dorothy would put her hand on her hip with a pained facial expression. In addition, at evaluation of her balance without an assistive device, Dorothy could stand on her left foot only momentarily, apparently because of pain in her back or hip with weight-bearing. Therefore, the therapist recommended that Dorothy use the cane consistently. She also continued to need reminders to keep her shoes tied and not walk on wet floors. In 4 more months, Dorothy could ascend and descend steps, execute car transfers, and even get up from the floor with only supervision and verbal and physical cues. She had not fallen at all.

Dorothy gradually became less interested in group exercise and often got up and left during a session. For that reason, and because of the level of independence Dorothy had achieved, maintenance therapy was discontinued.

DOCUMENTATION

If it's not written down, it didn't happen.

Complete, accurate documentation is important to demonstrate a patient's need for physical therapy to insurers and to others. The therapist must show how maintaining function and mobility is meaningful to the patient and the caregiver and how it is related to the services provided. Good documentation also protects the therapist in case of litigation. The following items constitute good documentation

- Physician orders—*PT consult,* or *evaluate and treat* (in most states)
- Initial evaluation—establish baseline, goals, and program
- Monthly reassessment
- Discharge summary—current status and reason for discharge
- Daily attendance logs
- Individual patient treatment records
- Progress notes—any change in patient condition or program

Information in evaluations and progress notes should be clear and understandable to a wide audience—other therapists who may treat the patient, nurses, physicians, attorneys, and reviewers, both from accrediting agencies and insurers. In managed care environments, a functional outcome must be meaningful, practical, and sustainable. Documentation is used to explain the implications of care to various user groups, including the purchaser of services (ie, the insurance company or health maintenance organization).

QUALITY ASSURANCE AND TOTAL QUALITY MANAGEMENT

Assessing quality in physical therapy, as in health care in general, began with quality assurance and has moved on to Continuous Quality Improvement (CQI) or Total Quality Management (TQM). These concepts, first developed for the manufacturing industry with the emphasis on cost containment, are being applied to the health care system.[4]

In industry, quality assurance systems often use review of structure and process to control costs and evaluate the quality of a product. The process evaluation approach can show ways to make a physical therapy department more productive and cost-efficient. However, in health care, optimal process does not always ensure optimal outcome.[5]

Traditionally, quality in health care has been assessed by measuring the content of the care given. This relates to the completeness of the evaluation, the appropriateness of treatment to diagnosis, and whether the treatment is relevant to the patient problems identified. Measuring outcomes is a more direct way of assessing quality of care. Previously discussed assessment tools of functional mobility can be used to provide reliable and valid outcomes measurement.

Jette discusses the use of health-related quality of life (HRQL) measures in physical therapy outcomes research.[6] HRQL includes a physical component (performance of daily activities required to sustain oneself); a psychologic component (cognitive, perceptual, and personality traits); and a social component (interaction of the individual within a larger social context).[7] Physical therapy outcomes relate primarily to the physical component. At present, however, these instruments are in the form of questionnaires or self-administered surveys. They are not applicable for patients with cognitive or emotional impairments, who cannot respond for themselves. In addition, these measures are too crude to be useful on the individual level needed for clinical use. The ideal HRQL instrument for use in the clinical practice of physical therapy has not yet been developed.[6]

QUALITY INDICATORS IN PHYSICAL THERAPY

Quality indicators involve the following four areas of assessment—structure, process, content, and outcome.

1. Structure involves the qualifications of staff and the physical facility, including safety of the department.
2. Process is concerned with how services are delivered; it involves efficiency and risk management.
3. Content involves the timeliness and appropriateness of care given and is measured by utilization review.
4. Outcome is the effectiveness of the service in meeting patient goals.[8]

THE CUSTOMER-ORIENTED MODEL

The customer-oriented model is a useful approach within the context of quality assurance.[9] This system involves the following steps

1. Identify the customers.
2. Determine the primary, reasonable, and valid expectations of the customers.
3. Decide your professional standards in dealing with these customers.
4. Define what you need to do to meet your customer expectations in accordance with your professional standards.
5. Choose what measures or indicators can be used to track performance to meet both customer expectations and professional standards.

Identifying the customer is the first task. There are external customers (outside the organization) and internal customers (fellow workers inside the organization).

External Customers

The most important customer in physical therapy is the patient who is being served. The patient's family, when involved, also are customers. Insurers and health maintenance organizations are becoming more important as purchasers of services for the patient. Other external customers are physicians and Joint Commission on Accreditation of Health Care Organizations or Medicare surveyors conducting periodic reviews.

Seeing patients as customers and determining their expectations is not an easy task for this population. Often patients are unable to express their expectations. However, during evaluation, physical therapy goals are identified. These are part of the physical function component of HRQL, including basic activities such as walking, dressing, and bathing. These goals, whether the patient can articulate them or not, are the greatest degree of functional independence possible within the person's abilities. The goals should be realistic and appropriate to the patient. The therapist needs to formulate goals, establish a sound recording and measurement system, and use a consistent method for evaluating the achievement of goals.[10] Typical maintenance goals include retaining the ability to walk 100 feet, the ability to propel and maneuver a wheelchair, or to don and doff shoes. One indicator of quality is meeting these individual patient goals.

A problem may arise when a patient meets some goals but not all. However, an overall assessment of functional status can be made. For each patient, determine if he has or has not met maintenance goals for the month; this becomes the quality indicator. This is an example of an outcome indicator.

To meet therapy goals, it is necessary for the patient to receive treatment regularly. Often patients miss therapy for various reasons. Counting the number of treatments scheduled by the department and comparing with actual treatments completed provides another indicator of quality. Further analysis can detect the reasons for missed treatments—both within and outside the control of the department. The reasons include patient illness, conflicts with other appointments, staff vacations, and inadequate staffing. This analysis can be helpful in finding procedures in both the physical therapy and nursing departments to ensure consistency in treatment. This is an indicator of process.

The patient's family may be considered a customer. When family members are in regular contact and express interest in the care of the patient, they should be contacted, their suggestions should be solicited, and they should be invited to call with any questions. These phone contacts, which are logged, can be conducted by the physical therapy aide or assistant. The indicator can be the phone log.

Physicians are important external customers; they may be an important source of referrals to the program. Physician expectations include prompt evaluation (eg, within 48 hours) and periodic (at least monthly) communication with the therapist concerning patient progress. These content indicators can be found in a chart review.

Outside reviewers review the safety and cleanliness of the department. The infection control manual and the policy and procedures handbook should be current and updated as needed, showing appropriate inspections and cleaning. A checklist for inspections can serve as the structure indicator. Inspectors also review charts to determine appropriateness and quality of care. Chart review for necessary documentation (eg, physician orders, initial evaluation, progress notes) can serve as a content indicator.

The purchaser or payer for services, an insurer or health maintenance organization, is becoming an ever more-important customer in emerging managed care systems. In managed care, unlike in fee-for-service systems, the emphasis is on the functional results rather than treatment of an impairment. Prevention of injury and further disability is important to minimize future costs to the system. The therapist must become skilled in predicting achievable desired outcomes and in developing ways to effectively prevent loss of function for the least amount of money.

Internal Customers

Internal customers include the nursing department, social work, facility administration, and co-workers. Nurses are very important members of the health care team. The therapist interacts directly and frequently with nurses, both formally (at team meetings) and informally. Expectations of nurses regarding physical therapy include clear communication of the treatment schedule and reporting observations of effects of treatment, especially untoward and unusual symptoms.

The social work department requires detailed information on a patient's functional status when home visits or discharge is planned. These communications can be documented in log form, in summaries of treatment team meetings, or in patient charts.

The expectations of administration regarding physical therapy include efficiency and safety. Efficiency can be crudely measured in the number of treatments per week or month and in analysis of the costs of treatment. Productivity indicators can be derived from a daily time analysis of the department. Time studies provide a valid estimate of productive and nonproductive times.[11] However, efficiency of the process does not consider factors outside the control of the department or the quality of the treatments given. Therefore, an outcome measurement must be performed. Productivity improvements must not be achieved at the expense of reducing quality of service.[12]

Sometimes the administration may not recognize additional ways in which the physical therapy department can contribute to the goals of the facility. These could include reducing the frequency of falls (facility liability) or reducing staff injuries (worker compensation claims). The therapist can address the problem of falls by assessing patients' fall risk, making environmental and patient recommendations, and conducting staff education. Prevention of staff injuries can be addressed with pre-employment screenings and staff instruction on lifting and moving patients. The therapist can explain to administration these additional roles. Indicators include the occurrence of falls and staff injuries.

SUGGESTED QUALITY INDICATORS

There are many possible quality indicators, depending on the area of assessment. Devices to measure the indicator may include the medical chart, phone logs, checklists, or summaries. What follows are suggested indicators, along with data sources.

Structure Indicators

Patient safety in physical therapy department	Inspection (eg, are patients monitored while in the department?)
Equipment safety	Equipment safety reports, inspection stickers
	Physical therapy inspection
Department cleanliness	Housekeeping inspection
	Dated cleaning list
Infection control	Physical therapy inspection
	Whirlpool cultures
Staff qualifications	Copies of licensure, continuing education units, training certificate

Process Indicators

Efficiency	Time-study analysis (patients per day per therapist)
Risk and complication factors	Incident reports
	Infection rates
Patient attendance	Attendance records
	Number of and reasons for missed appointments
Interdisciplinary focus	Treatment team summaries
	Program notes
	Phone logs

Content Indicators

Initial evaluation complete	Peer chart review
Relevant data in progress notes	Peer chart review
Treatment plan relevant to therapy goals	Peer chart review

Outcomes Indicators

Documented maintenance and improvement in functional tasks	Interdisciplinary chart review
Health-related quality of life	Patient questionnaires
Patient satisfaction	Patient or family surveys

After an indicator and the device to measure it are selected, set a threshold. Performance below the threshold triggers additional analysis. If the criterion is met at 100 percent every month, the chances are that indicator is not a problem for the department and can be set aside, at least temporarily. If the indicator is never met, there may be a problem, or perhaps that indicator is not appropriate for the department.

Structure, process, and content are inward-looking. These indicators enforce a baseline standard of safety, efficiency, and documentation for the department. Outcome measurement is outward-looking. Do the patients benefit? Are they meeting important and realistic goals? Does therapy help?

SUMMARY

There is support for research in the area of outcome assessment. The best way to measure the outcome of rehabilitation of an older person depends on the health problem, the setting, and the way the data are used.[13] Increasingly in the future physical therapists will need to measure outcomes to prove the effectiveness of various physical therapy interventions and will need to develop cost-effective methods of providing services.

REFERENCES

1. Code of Federal Regulations (revised Oct 1, 1992) 42 CFR 409.33 (c)–(5).
2. Lewis CB, Ellis A, Wagner M. Drugs and the elderly patient. *Clin Manage Phys* 1992;12:54–64.
3. Ciccone, CD: *Pharmacology in rehabilitation*. Philadelphia: Davis, 1990.
4. Hunter SJ, Olsen B, Stewart L. TQM in PT. *PT Mag Phys Ther* 1993;1:54–8, 85.
5. Brook RH, Appel FA. Quality-of-care assessment: Choosing a method for peer review. *N Engl J Med* 1973;288:1323–1329.
6. Jette AM. Using health-related quality of life measures in physical therapy outcomes research. *Phys Ther* 1993;73:528–536.
7. Engle G. The biopsychosocial model and medical education. *N Engl J Med* 1982;306:802–806.
8. American Physical Therapy Association. *Quality assurance: An APTA Practice Management Publication*. Alexandria, VA: APTA, 1990.
9. Tenner AR, Detoro IJ. *Total quality management: Three steps to continuous improvement*. Reading, MA: Addison-Wesley, 1992.
10. Wilson E, Davis C, Firth G, Greenham D, Puri C. Measuring effectiveness in the physiotherapy dept. *Dimens Health Serv* 1990;67(1):15–17.
11. American Physical Therapy Association. *Productivity in Physical Therapy-Resource Guide*. Alexandria, VA: APTA, 1983.
12. Ratinaud JP. Physical therapy productivity: Efficiency? Effectiveness? or both? *Clin Manage Phys Ther* 1984;4(4):12–14.
13. Studenski S, Duncan PW. Measuring rehabilitation outcomes. *Clin Geriatr Med* 1993;9:823–829.

10

Conclusion

PSYCHOLOGIC BENEFITS

A regular program of exercise may help the older person increase or maintain his strength, range of motion, and mobility. There are also other benefits associated with exercise. People just seem to feel better after exercise. Temporary improvements lasting 2 to 5 hours have been shown in levels of anxiety, depression, and self-esteem in response to physical activity.[1–5] In fact, the benefits of exercise for those with anxiety or depression are comparable to what can be achieved with psychotherapy.[6]

Regular exercise is effective nondrug therapy for stress, sleep disorders, depression, and anxiety, as well as for chronic conditions of aging.[7]

People also seem to enjoy the socialization that attends group activities. They become more interested in others, self-preoccupation declines, and real friendships develop.

ECONOMIC VALUE OF PREVENTION

Helping a patient retain functional abilities improves her quality of life. Maximizing a patient's independence with activities of daily living saves money and staff time. A program that prevents falls saves health care dollars otherwise spent on injuries.

M. Joycelyn Elders, M.D., former Surgeon General of the United States Public Health Service, is a physical therapist. In an interview in October 1993, she said, "We've got to refocus our attention toward thinking about prevention, and, to me, physical therapy is a means of both preventing a disability from occurring and markedly decreasing it once it has occurred . . . I want to change the way we think about health by putting prevention first."[8]

AMERICAN PHYSICAL THERAPY ASSOCIATION POSITION

The American Physical Therapy Association (APTA), which represents more than 65,000 physical therapists, physical therapist assistants, and students, in a statement on health care reform recommended osteoporosis and arthritis prevention programs and programs aimed at decreasing falls among the elderly. It also recommended that a standard benefit package "include coverage for attaining and maintaining function and preventing deterioration. Without these services, patient conditions will deteriorate and result in the need for more costly health care in the future."[9]

Marilyn Moffat, P.T. Ph.D., President of the APTA, stated that "Regardless of the type of health care system that arises during the next few years, resources will be decreased and physical therapists will need to devise innovative ways to deliver care."[10]

SUMMARY

The goals for the exercise programs outlined are to sustain the highest level of mobility for every patient and to promote independence, autonomy, and dignity; to prevent falls, injuries, and accidents without the use of restraints; and to improve overall quality of life for the elderly. There is evidence that maintenance therapy can improve the quality of life and decrease the cost of care for those who must reside in institutions.[11] The group programs suggested provide a means to deliver services in a cost-effective way, require a minimum of equipment, and can be carried out by a person who receives training on the job and with periodic supervision by a therapist. New health care initiatives present challenges—and opportunities—to show that it is cost-effective and humane to provide preventive services to residents of long-term care facilities, as well as those in the community, who are at risk for disability.

REFERENCES

1. Pickles B. Biological aspect of aging. *Clin Phys Ther* 1989;21:27–76.
2. Morgan WP. Affective beneficence of vigorous physical activity. *Med Sci Sports Exerc* 1985;17:94–100.
3. Raglin JS, Morgan WP. Influence of exercise and quiet rest on state anxiety and blood pressure. *Med Sci Sports Exerc* 1987;19:456-463.
4. Thirlaway K, Benton D. Participation in physical activity and cardiovascular fitness have different effects on mental health and mood. *J Psychosom Res* 1992;36:657–665.
5. Byrne A, Byrne DG. The effect of exercise on depression, anxiety and other mood states: A review. *J Psychosom Res* 1993;37:565–574.
6. Raglin JS. Exercise and mental health: Beneficial and detrimental effects. *Sports Med* 1990;9:323–329.

7. Kligman EW, Pepin E. Prescribing physical activity for older patients. *Geriatrics* 1992;47(8):33–34,37–44,47.

8. Colan BJ. Joycelyn Elders remembers physical therapy influence. *Adv Phys Ther* 1993;4(41):3–4.

9. American Physical Therapy Association. Statement on health care reform: Summary of key issues. *PT Mag Phys Ther* 1994;2:19–26.

10. Moffat M. President's message on PT education. *PT Mag Phys Ther* 1993;1(11):41–42.

11. Joseph CL, Wanless W. Rehabilitation in the nursing home. *Clin Geriatr Med* 1993;9:859–871.

A

Guarding, Assistance, Cues

GUARDING

Close contact guard   The patient requires two-hand contact for balance assistance and safety. Depending on the size and strength of the person assisting relative to the patient's size, the patient is prevented from falling, or descent to the floor is controlled.

Contact guard   The patient requires one-hand contact for safety. The patient is prevented from falling, or descent to the floor is controlled.

Close supervision   The patient requires a person within an arm's length who can move in quickly to prevent an injurious fall.

Far supervision   The patient is observed while performing the activity.

Independent   Another person is not required for the activity.

ASSISTANCE

Minimal assistance   The patient provides more than 75 percent of the strength needed to perform the activity.

Moderate assistance   The patient provides 50 to 75 percent of the strength needed to perform the activity.

Maximal assistance   The patient provides less than 50 percent of the strength needed to perform the activity.

Dependent   The patient requires total assistance for the activity.

CUING

Verbal cues   The patient is instructed or reminded of correct technique just before or during the movement.

Physical cues   The patient requires a light touch on the part to be moved to indicate the direction of movement requested.

Demonstration   The patient is shown the requested movement just before being asked to move.

B

Disablement Terminology

Disease   The intrinsic pathology or disorder.

Impairment   Loss or abnormality of psychologic, physiologic, or anatomic structure or function at organ level.

Disability   Restriction or lack of ability to perform an activity in a normal manner.

Handicap   Disadvantage due to impairment or disability that limits or prevents fulfillment of a normal role (depends on age, sex, sociocultural factors) for the person.

(Adapted from International Classification of Impairments, Disabilities and Handicaps. Geneva: World Health Organization 1980)

C

Joint Range of Motion

1. The anatomic position of an extremity is accepted as 0 degrees.
2. The terms *extension* and *hyperextension* are differentiated from one another. *Extension* is used when the motion opposite to flexion at the 0-degree starting position is a natural motion. *Hyperextension* is used when the motion opposite to flexion at the 0-degree starting position is an unnatural one.
3. Limited motion is expressed in degrees of flexion (or extension) available from the 0-degree starting position, or as a flexion (or extension) contracture (or deformity).

(Adapted from Joint Motion: Method of Measuring and Recording. Chicago: American Academy of Orthopedic Surgeons 1965)

D

Five-point Scale for Grading Muscles

5 = Normal strength
4 = Ability to resist against gravity and moderate resistance throughout range of motion
3 = Ability to move through full range of motion against gravity
2 = Ability to move through full range of motion with gravity eliminated
1 = A flicker of movement is seen or felt in the muscle
0 = No contraction palpable

*Note: In muscle testing, weakness must be differentiated from restriction in range of motion.

(Adapted from Daniels L, Worthingham C. *Muscle testing: techniques of manual examination*, 5th ed. Philadelphia: Saunders, 1986)

Index